SpringerBriefs in Business

For further volumes:
http://www.springer.com/series/8860

Dieter Ahlert · Benjamin Schefer

Vertical Price Coordination and Brand Care

Interdisciplinary Perspectives on the Prohibition of Resale Price Maintenance

Springer

Dieter Ahlert
Benjamin Schefer
Department of Retailing
and Network Marketing
University of Münster
Münster
Germany

ISSN 2191-5482 ISSN 2191-5490 (electronic)
ISBN 978-3-642-35569-1 ISBN 978-3-642-35570-7 (eBook)
DOI 10.1007/978-3-642-35570-7
Springer Heidelberg New York Dordrecht London

Library of Congress Control Number: 2013933301

Printed on acid-free paper

Springer is part of Springer Science+Business Media (www.springer.com)

Contents

Chapter 1
Introduction to the Current Problem

Cartel-law intervention is intended to prevent restraints of competition, not to cause them. Therefore, for *all regulations governing freedom of action in business*, the universally acknowledged principle applies that they *must be reviewed with a view to de-regulation at regular intervals*.[1] There is an acute need for review particularly when—as in the case of coordinated price management between manufacturing and retailing—the enforcement by the authorities of restrictive legal provisions may be tightened up further. However, groups of experts at national and international levels, at the same time, disagree increasingly as to whether such legal restrictions can be justified in terms of the underlying principle. There is a risk that any further restriction of freedom to contract will tend to stifle innovation and competitive diversity rather than sustainably improve consumer welfare.

In January 2010, one of the largest investigations in the history of the Federal Cartel Office (Germany) caused considerable uproar. This occurred not only in the food sector but also generally in the consumer-goods sector—at the latest with similar investigations at mattress companies. Manufacturers and distributors were suspected of collusion with regard to the formation of final consumer prices. In an explanatory recommendation document[2] and at numerous information events and in press publications, the Federal Cartel Office made it clear that not merely classic 'resale price maintenance', but all conceivable forms of vertical price and brand care within the value chain may be risky for cartel-law purposes, even if they are only remotely concerned with coordinated pricing.

This raises the question of whether *vertical price coordination within a value chain*, as seen from the perspective of competition or welfare economics, is

---

[1] Cf. on the mode of operation of such a test bench in the field of conflict between regulation and deregulation Müller (2003) and Ahlert et al. (1988), pp. V f.

[2] The Federal Cartel Office (Germany) has published, as a guide for the companies affected by the investigation of vertical price agreements, a provisional evaluation referred to as a recommendation (*Handreichung*) which distinguishes between clearly prohibited situations and practices possibly to be classified as critical. The content of the "Handreichung" of particular relevance for the subject matter of our investigation can be seen in *Annex 1* of this article.

D. Ahlert and B. Schefer, *Vertical Price Coordination and Brand Care*,
SpringerBriefs in Business, DOI: 10.1007/978-3-642-35570-7_1,

fundamentally capable of causing severe negative effects that justify high fines as in the case of horizontal price cartels. If this is not the case per se, but *only in exceptional cases* (under certain conditions), the next question that arises is whether cartel law as it currently applies should be amended.[3] This question extends to restrictive legal provisions[4] and the practical intervention of the cartel authorities, as well as to case law in Germany and in the EU. The question arises in particular whether it can be shown that vertical price coordination in the normal case does not inhibit the operation of horizontal processes of competition (i.e. inter-brand competition). To the contrary, it can help to eliminate distortions of competition (market failure).

The obviously stricter approach of cartel-law practice is not undisputed from the perspective of business practice and management theory.[5] Some marketing experts point out the following problems: cartel-law intervention may be *aimed at* vertical price maintenance, but it *impacts* on almost all modern vertical-marketing tools and strategies to the extent to which these *could*, even if merely indirectly, have any bearing on vertical price management.[6] There is already talk of considerable collateral damage in business practice.

Particularly criticised by competition law is the *exchange of information along the value chain* (extending beyond mere business exchange between suppliers and their sales agents). This applies firstly to the modern IT-aided forms of cost-effective data exchange insofar as they (*could*) include so-called price-sensitive data. Also affected are the strategic coordination of the market-launch concepts of manufacturing and retailing at the consumer level and, resulting from the same processes, the explicit formulation of mutual expectations of the conduct of business partners with respect to brand positioning ('strategic brand coordination'). This is because brand positioning without price positioning is inconceivable.

---

[3] Cf. also as examples the articles by Haucap and Klein (2012), Schwalbe (2012), and Wey (2012).

[4] The 7th amendment of the German Act against Restraints of Competition [*Gesetz gegen Wettbewerbsbeschränkungen* (hereinafter "GWB")] of 1 July 2005 radically changed German cartel law and adapted it to European cartel law. This led to the abolition of the express prohibition of vertical price fixing (as per sec. 14 GWB former version). Pertinent legal provisions, in which the resale price maintenance prohibition (hereinafter referred to as 'RPM prohibition' for short) is entrenched, are secs. 1 and 2 GWB, Art. 101 TFEU and, additionally, the new Vertical Block Exemption Regulation of the European Commission which came into force on 1 June 2010 and the guidelines for vertical restraints published thereon of 10 May 2010. If the RPM prohibition were to be abolished, this would require amendment of several provisions of German and European cartel law. Also relevant to our analysis are the unilateral use of so-called 'pressure and incentives to enforce vertical restraints' [sec. 21 (2) GWB] and "inequitable obstruction in value systems" (sec. 20 GWB); here, in particular, so-called passive discrimination (granting of advantages without objectively justified reason, sec. 20 (3) GWB) (translated from German).

[5] Cf. as examples also the articles by Greipl (2012), Kenning and Wobker (2012), Lademann (2012), Mocken (2012), Sanktjohanser (2012), Schröder (2012) and Olbrich and Grewe (2012).

[6] More information on this in Ahlert et al. (2011) and the literature specified therein.

Surprisingly, *projects involving cooperation between manufacturing and retailing*, especially vertical category management, are also increasingly viewed with suspicion. They appear suspicious to some 'trust-busters', because it would be naive to assume that the subject of vertical price structuring could be wholly excluded from value partnerships (efficient consumer response). It seems at least unlikely that, with a partnership atmosphere within the value system, one of the participants would pursue a loss-leader policy, sell-off campaigns or conduct brand vandalism in the relevant goods category.

Even the more recent approaches towards a close interaction of manufacturing and retailing enterprises in the area of *interactive innovation management* are inconceivable without any express agreement on prices. At the same time, it is not only a matter of generating and implementing innovative services, more efficient logistics and distribution processes and more effective forms of coordinated brand communications within the value chain, but also increasingly a matter of marketing complete problem-solving concepts, i.e. 'solution selling'.[7] Innovative supply concepts, emerging from multi-level business cooperation or virtual networks, inevitably contain new kinds of price-performance combination. Responding to them with competition-law reservations could, to a certain extent, have the effect of stifling diversity.

The current discussion is not, therefore, solely concerned with vertical resale price maintenance, but is much wider and encompasses the diverse range of measures and strategies in the sales channels of the consumer-goods economy, which nowadays operate under the term *vertical price and brand care*.[8]

The increasingly strict enforcement by the authorities of the restrictive provisions of cartel law in vertical marketing is also the subject of controversy in the jurisprudence field.[9] For example, the theory is held that German cartel-law practice has departed itself from the international position held by some countries (e.g. of the USA, in some cases also the EU).[10] The abolition by the Supreme Court of the per-se prohibition of minimum-price agreements in the USA (2007) and the new European Commission guidelines on vertical restraints (2010) which, in a few cases of practical relevance, tend to evaluate vertical price agreements as positive, have revived a decade-old interdisciplinary discussion:

There is a general question as to whether State intervention in the vertical value-adding processes is compatible with the underlying principle of effective competition.

---

[7] Cf. as an overview Kawohl (2010).

[8] Cf. for the definition and typology of 'vertical price and brand care' the article by Schefer in *Annex II*.

[9] Cf. for examples the articles by Blechman (2012), Glowik (2012), Möschel (2012) and Simon (2012).

[10] Especially to the point, Möschel (2010).

The *controversial discussion conducted to date* exhibits the following main characteristics:

1. The discussion centres almost exclusively on the *prohibition of inflexible fixed-price maintenance systems*. However, these are neither widespread nor desired in business practice. On the contrary; according to the latest empirical surveys from *Institute of Retailing and Network Marketing at the University of Muenster*, there is no significant interest in reverting to such antiquated strategies of vertical marketing, neither in the industries that rely on branding nor in major retailing systems. Owing to their lack of flexibility and high costs, classical reverse systems of resale price maintenance are rejected out of hand in practice.

   Business practice is, in many cases, concerned only with the fundamental admissibility of *a multi-level harmonisation of price and brand management within the value chain*. This refers, for example, to open discussions on targeted brand-policy price architectures in sales channels, but also to price-care measures which are not the subject of a multilateral, but rather of a bilateral or individual agreement. These include agreements of limited duration on price ranges and special-offers.

   However, the majority of articles on competition economy—similar to those recently published in the book containing the original German version of this article[11]—make no distinction, in assuming negative effects on competition, between classic fixed-price maintenance systems and multi-facetted forms of vertical price and brand maintenance. The English language literature usually talks generally of RPM ("resale price maintenance"). Where price-care measures—also referred to as "soft price maintenance"—are even considered worthy of separate examination, they are frequently given the same negative evaluation as inflexible price restraints. This occurs not infrequently on the grounds that they may mean nothing other than the introduction of vertical (fixed) price maintenance 'by the back door'.

   Recommended retail prices which, in the past, if considered in greater detail,[12] were largely regarded as unobjectionable,[13] represent an exception to this tendency to equate the phenomena. Nevertheless, these are also currently regarded increasingly with suspicion in cartel-law practice.
2. When deducing effects harmful to competition, attention is paid one-sidedly to the inflexible price restraints that apply uniformly to all intermediaries, but these are also assumed, equally one-sidedly, on the basis exclusively of extreme scenarios of inflexible and fossilised market structures. It is assumed, therefore, that *market failure* already exists. Normally, no attempt is made to examine

[11] Cf. Ahlert et al. (2012) and the articles by Haucap and Klein (2012), Schwalbe (2012) and Wey (2012).

[12] Cf. Wey (2012) as an example: 'If one looks at the literature on price recommendations, one will be surprised to note that there is almost nothing of relevance on this topic'.

[13] Cf. also the detailed article by Greipl (2012).

whether negative effects on competition of vertical price coordination are also observed in markets which distinguish themselves (at least to a large extent) by *effective competitive processes*.

3. Price restraints are normally exposed as an 'ambivalent phenomenon' and it is assumed that they can be appropriately assessed for competition-policy purposes by comparing—i.e. netting—their *positive and negative effects on competition or welfare*.[14] However, the positive effects of price maintenance are usually not judged as being so favourable[15] as to compensate for the negative effects for fixed-price maintenance systems. Often, the consequence is then to argue in favour of retaining strict, blanket RPM prohibition.

In our view, the routine arguments outlined above do not represent a suitable basis on which to examine the need for deregulation in conformity with the guiding principle. For this reason, the following discussion is based on a *different course of action*:

The starting point is the finding that there is no need to prove *positive* effects of RPM on competition or welfare in order to justify their admissibility. As expression of the freedom of contract entrenched in the German Basic Law, RPM is a priori legitimate. The retention of the hitherto blanket (non-differentiated) RPM prohibition could, therefore, only be justified if two requirements were met,

- *Firstly*, that price-maintenance systems, if they were admissible, (could) generally and causally impair the effectiveness of competition *and*,
- *Secondly*, that the blanket prohibition of all vertical price coordination did not involve even greater potential risk to the effectiveness of competition.

Re 1: If price maintenance, contrary to this assumed effect, does not have a general but merely a partial distorting potential, i.e. only in a few specific cases, must prohibition be restricted to just these exceptional cases. Hereinafter, this postulation will be referred to as a *'case-by-case approach'*.[16] There is also cause to inquire as to whether price maintenance in these cases is even responsible for *causing* market failure or whether it is more an accompanying *symptom* of other causal factors (normally insurmountable barriers to market entry). Competition-policy intervention should aim at the causes and not at the symptoms.

---

[14] The guidelines of the European Commission on vertical restraints from 2010 (hereinafter referred to as 'Vertical GL'), paragraph 5: 'Article 101 provides a legal framework for the assessment of vertical restraints, which takes into consideration the distinction between anti-competitive and pro-competitive effects. Article 101(1) prohibits those agreements which appreciably restrict or distort competition, while Article 101(3) exempts those agreements which confer sufficient benefits to outweigh the anti-competitive effects.' This method of balancing the positive effects of price restraints against the negative also reflects the more recent case law on vertical restraints in the USA. Cf. Blechman (2012).

[15] Particularly clear, Simon (2012) and Wey (2012).

[16] At the symposium in Münster on 27 January 2011, some competition economists expressed support for the 'case-by-case approach' of a differentiated evaluation of price maintenance systems. Cf. also the articles by Haucap and Klein (2012) and Schwalbe (2012).

Re 2: This aspect has tended to be neglected until now and, for this reason, is the focal point of this article. The individual aspects of the considerable overall *collateral damage of a blanket RPM prohibition* will be shown and why the increasingly strict enforcement of these restrictive legal provisions by the authorities must be seen as *one of the greatest potential risks of the present time for the entire consumer goods industry.*

The effects on competition or welfare must be weighed up in conformity with the guiding principle in the review for (de)-regulation in such a way that the negative effects of admissible RPM and the negative effects of the RPM prohibition[17] are compared with each other. To this end, both assumed effects must not only be plausible but also explainable in terms of competition theory.

The *implications for competition policy* are then as follows:

- If the first-mentioned negative effects do not significantly exceed the last-mentioned *in any conceivable case*, it would be logical to call for the *abolition of this prohibition provision* (by making a new statute).
- If the first-mentioned negative effects significantly exceed the last-mentioned *only in certain cases*, the *partial retention of this prohibition provision* limited to these clearly defined cases must be considered.
- Since, in the two above-mentioned cases, the necessary changes in German and European competition law are likely to take a long time, but retaining the regulation currently gives rise to great risks, *a less restrictive interpretation and application of the existing legal provisions* on the part of the competition authorities and the courts in the interim period—to the extent of the scope of discretion permitted by applicable law—would be desirable for competition-policy reasons. Consideration should be given in particular to freedom of action in vertical price and brand maintenance.

Given the concise nature of the discussion required here, arguments can only be sketched out. For more information and a scientific basis, we refer to the more detailed presentation in our *economic manifesto on the deregulation of consumer-goods distribution.*[18] The competition-policy principle underlying the present article, the *construct of effective competition*, is also explained in more detail therein.

From the marketing perspective, attention is also drawn to the following misunderstanding: A person who *opposes the prohibition* of price maintenance does *not necessarily favour* price maintenance as a means of vertical marketing. Moreover, abolishing this prohibiting provision is unlikely to lead to a situation in which price maintenance is introduced en masse or entire branches of industry immediately become "tainted" by inflexible fixed-price maintenance systems.[19]

---

[17] Negative effects of the RPM prohibition are not the same as (any) positive effects of admissible price restraints. The former may occur when no positive effects whatsoever are evident for price restraints or their introduction is not even intentional. This finding may appear to split hairs, but it is of fundamental importance. More on this in Chap. 3.

[18] Cf. Ahlert et al. (2011).

[19] Cf. Sect. 5.1 for details.

The problems typical for cooperation systems described in detail in the literature on cooperation theory, i.e. free-riders, saboteurs and other free-loaders[20] could more easily be dealt with merely as a result of the widened *possibilities* of effective price and brand care.

In order to make this argument heard, it is intended in Chap. 2 first of all to eliminate the *misconception that vertical price and brand care per se diminishes consumer welfare* or even indicates a conspiracy of manufacturing and retailing against the consumer. The serious *risks to the effectiveness of competition arising from the prohibition of price maintenance* will then be shown systematically in Chap. 3. The hypotheses regarding the *potentially negative effects on competition of admissible price restraints* will be presented and critically reviewed in Chap. 4. On the basis of these analyses which show that, in many cases, if not even as a rule, competition is restricted to a much greater extent by RPM prohibition than by admissible price restraints, the *implications for competition policy* will be concluded in Chap. 5.

References

Ahlert D (ed) (1981) Vertragliche Vertriebssysteme zwischen Industrie und Handel. Grundzüge einer betriebswirtschaftlichen, rechtlichen und volkswirtschaftlichen Beurteilung, Wiesbaden

Ahlert D, Grossekettler H, Sandrock O (1988) Vorwort der Herausgeber zur Schriftenreihe Marketing/Recht/Wettbewerb. In: Ahlert D (ed) Marketing-Rechts-Management, Cologne inter alia, pp 5–7

Ahlert D (1996) Distributionspolitik, 3rd edn., Stuttgart

Ahlert D, Kenning P, Schröder H, Olbrich R (2012) (eds) Vertikale Preis- und Markenpflege im Kreuzfeuer des Kartellrechts, Wiesbaden

Ahlert D, Kenning P, Schröder H, Olbrich R (2011) Vielfalt durch Gestaltungsfreiheit im Wettbewerb. Ein ökonomisches Manifest zur Deregulierung der Konsumgüterdistribution, Munich

Blechman M (2012) Unreasonable Restraints of Trade. Die Entwicklung der Rechtsprechung zum Preisbindungsverbot in den USA. In: Ahlert D, Kenning P, Schröder H, Olbrich R (eds) Vertikale Preis- und Markenpflege im Kreuzfeuer des Kartellrechts, Wiesbaden, pp 199–204

Glowik J (2012) Das große Schweigen—oder dient ein offener Diskurs zwischen Handel und Industrie den Interessen der Verbraucher? Einige Denkanstöße aus der Praxis. In: Ahlert D, Kenning P, Schröder H, Olbrich R (eds) Vertikale Preis- und Markenpflege im Kreuzfeuer des Kartellrechts, Wiesbaden, pp 243–248

Greipl E (2012) Retail Brand-Politik. Die Funktion des Markenartikels. In: Ahlert D, Kenning P, Schröder H, Olbrich R (eds) Vertikale Preis- und Markenpflege im Kreuzfeuer des Kartellrechts, Wiesbaden, pp 211–220

Haucap J, Klein G (2012) Einschränkungen der Preisgestaltung im Einzelhandel aus wettbewerbsökonomischer Perspektive. In: Ahlert D, Kenning P, Schröder H, Olbrich R (eds) Vertikale Preis- und Markenpflege im Kreuzfeuer des Kartellrechts, Wiesbaden, pp 169–186

---

[20] More information on this in Ahlert (1981, pp. 63ff), (1996, pp. 123ff) and the literature specified therein.

Kawohl JM (2010) Lösungsorientierung von Handelsunternehmen. Konzeption und Erfolgsmessung, Wiesbaden

Kenning P, Wobker I (2012) Die negativen Folgen von Kundenverwirrtheit und die moderierende Rolle von Vertrauen in der Konsumgüterdistribution. Konzeptionelles Modell und empirische Befunde. In: Ahlert D, Kenning P, Schröder H, Olbrich R (eds) Vertikale Preis- und Markenpflege im Kreuzfeuer des Kartellrechts, Wiesbaden, pp 69–94

Lademann RP (2012) Die ökonomischen Aspekte der Preisempfehlung im Lichte von Besonderheiten der Ernährungswirtschaft. In: Ahlert D, Kenning P, Schröder H, Olbrich R (eds) Vertikale Preis-und Markenpflege im Kreuzfeuer des Kartellrechts, Wiesbaden, pp 233–242

Mocken W (2012) Integrierte Markenführerschaft. Vertriebskooperation zwischen Industrie und Handel. In Ahlert D, Kenning P, Schröder H, Olbrich R (eds) Vertikale Preis- und Markenpflege im Kreuzfeuer des Kartellrechts, Wiesbaden, pp 227–232

Möschel W (2010) Markenartikel und vertikale Kooperation. In: Wirtschaft und Wettbewerb, no 12, pp 1229–1237

Möschel W (2012) Zwecke der Preisempfehlung. Die Motive des Gesetzgebers. In: Ahlert D, Kenning P, Schröder H, Olbrich R (eds) Vertikale Preis- und Markenpflege im Kreuzfeuer des Kartellrechts, Wiesbaden, pp 193–198

Müller CA (2003) (De-) Regulierung und Unternehmertum, St. Gallen

Olbrich R, Grewe G (2012) Vertikale Vertriebssysteme und rechtliche Regulierung der vertikalen Preispflege in Europa. Zu den Begründungszusammenhängen, zur Ungleichbehandlung der Systeme und zu den Konsequenzen für den Konsumgütersektor. In: Ahlert D, Kenning P, Schröder H, Olbrich R (eds) Vertikale Preis- und Markenpflege im Kreuzfeuer des Kartellrechts, Wiesbaden, pp 95–126

Sanktjohanser J (2012) Kooperation zwischen Industrie und Handel. Eine Stellungnahme des HDE zur Handreichung des Bundeskartellamtes. In: Ahlert D, Kenning P, Schröder H, Olbrich R (eds) Vertikale Preis-und Markenpflege im Kreuzfeuer des Kartellrechts, Wiesbaden, pp 205–210

Schröder H (2012) Category Management in der Gruppenfreistellungsverordnung 2010—eine Gefahr für die cooperative Markenführung. In: Ahlert D, Kenning P, Schröder H, Olbrich R (eds) Vertikale Preis- und Markenpflege im Kreuzfeuer des Kartellrechts, Wiesbaden, pp 127–154

Schwalbe U (2012) Wettbewerbsökonomische Aspekte der Preisbindung in Wertschöpfungsketten. In: Ahlert D, Kenning P, Schröder H, Olbrich R (eds) Vertikale Preis- und Markenpflege im Kreuzfeuer des Kartellrechts, Wiesbaden, pp 155–168

Simon S (2012) Preisbindungen und Preisempfehlungen. Kartellrechtliche Grenzen der vertikalen Kooperation zwischen Industrie und Handel. In: Ahlert D, Kenning P, Schröder H, Olbrich R (eds) Vertikale Preis- und Markenpflege im Kreuzfeuer des Kartellrechts, Wiesbaden, pp 249–256

Wey C (2012) Preisempfehlungen aus wettbewerbsökonomischer Sicht. In: Ahlert D, Kenning P, Schröder H, Olbrich R (eds) Vertikale Preis-und Markenpflege im Kreuzfeuer des Kartellrechts, Wiesbaden, pp 221–226

Chapter 2
The Myth that Welfare is Promoted by Prohibiting Vertical Price and Brand Maintenance

The misconception that it is only necessary to fight price maintenance in order to guarantee the supply at favourable prices to consumers of the desired branded goods is widespread among the public and, surprisingly, also among students of economics. For example, a snap poll involving 193 participants, (mainly students aged between 20 and 36 years) by the Muenster Institute of Retailing and Network Marketing in 2010 revealed a considerable lack of knowledge of the topic of vertical price management (cf. Fig. 2.1).

If the advocates of cartel-law practice had to present themselves for public election at regular intervals, they would be well advised to adhere to strict RPM prohibition. The year-long discussion on price maintenance has obviously caused the subject of price-maintenance prohibition to become taboo and any attempt to change the situation is doomed to failure.

2.1 Starting Point: What Gives Rise to Optimum Consumer Welfare?

In our view, consumers experience the *greatest conceivable degree of welfare* when the effectiveness of competition is permanently guaranteed. Undisputed is the fact that this refers to competition *between* different supply concepts and brands. It is, therefore, a matter of the *effectiveness of inter-brand competition*. This presupposes supply diversity. Well-proven and innovative selling efforts compete with each other for the favour of consumers. Value systems in the consumer-goods sector normally have multiple levels with manufacturers and distributors being involved in marketing efforts. The most attractive supply concepts usually feature a harmonious combination of excellent services from both manufacturers and distributors. Conflicts *within* such service combinations, no matter

D. Ahlert and B. Schefer, *Vertical Price Coordination and Brand Care*, SpringerBriefs in Business, DOI: 10.1007/978-3-642-35570-7_2,

- More than 55% of respondents believed that manufacturers themselves set the selling prices of their products in retailing.
- On average, those asked estimate that 40–60 per cent of the products available in the most important consumer-goods sectors are price-maintained.
- 50 per cent regard a controlling influence of the manufacturer on the price structure of the distributor as negative.
- More than 54 per cent consider that price maintenance is disadvantageous to consumers.
- 60 per cent support a strict prohibition of every form of price fixing between manufacturing and retailing.
- 35 per cent subscribe to the theory that manufacturers and distributors increasingly conspire against consumers. In many cases, stricter action against value-adding partnerships is even welcomed, because it is widely believed that the strict prohibition of price and brand care leads to falling prices and, therefore raises consumer welfare.

Fig. 2.1 Results from a poll by University of Muenster, 2010

whether they concern brand communications or strategic price positioning, may confuse the consumer and impair his faith in the quality.[1]

Therefore: Diversity presupposes freedom of contract and of action in sales channels.

However, if industrial and commercial enterprises are increasingly prohibited by cartel law from avoiding consumer confusion by undertaking the necessary price and brand care, this may endanger strong brands and destroy incentives to innovate.

2.2 How do Strong Brands Arise and How do They Raise Welfare?

In order to justify for the above-mentioned theories, it is necessary to make a brief *excursion into the more modern theory of the formation of strong brands.*[2] Brands are created inside human minds; they cannot be ‘made’. Anyone attempting to burn his brand onto peoples minds by force ‘cowboy-style’ is certainly destined to fail. These are the results of our neuroscientific research at the University of Muenster. Strong brands are based on myths. A particularly graphic example of this is Red Bull, one of the few products that became a strong brand within a truly short period

---

[1] Cf. also the detailed article of Kenning and Wobker (2012).

[2] Cf. for the overview Ahlert (2004); Ahlert et al. (2006b) and Zernisch (2004).

27 guests attending a birthday party and aged between 23 and 68 participated in a blind test. In two experiments, the guests sampled two glasses each of sparkling wine (so called 'Sekt') in direct comparison and then immediately attempted to name the 'Sekt' that they personally found tasted best. The test persons were not told what brand they were just drinking. In casual conversation with the host, however, they were informed of the (alleged) price for the bottle of the relevant sparkling wine purchased from a distributor. What the participants did not know: all glasses contained the same brand of sparkling wine.

Results:

Experiment (1)
7 participants selected the 'Sekt' for € 2.99, 15 participants the 'Sekt' for € 4.99, 5 were undecided

Experiment (2)
10 participants chose the 'Sekt' for € 6.99, 10 participants the 'Sekt' for € 10.95, 7 were undecided

A similar result was obtained in a comparable experiment performed with wine (cf. Plassmann et al. 2008, p. 1050 ff.).The researchers explained it with the aid of a brain scan of the participating test persons (the exact method is called functional magnetic resonance imaging: see Ahlert/Hubert 2010, p. 47ff. for further details).
It could be proven that the change in price influences neural correlates of taste processing. In other words, the test persons did not merely think that the more expensive wine tasted better to them, this was really the case.

Fig. 2.2 Blind test with sparkling wine (University of Muenster 2010) [Cf. Schefer (2013) (forthcoming)]

of time. Red Bull is not a product essential to life. The consumer can avoid the product if he is confused by the consistently high price. After all, there are many alternative cult products and the consumer can also refrain from buying altogether.

But what would happen in the consumer's mind if the price of Red Bull was suddenly radically reduced?

A 'magic potion' for a discount price? 'Supernatural powers' for the same price as still mineral water? Price destruction would result in people ceasing to appreciate Red Bull and it would no longer have the effects attributed to it for the well-being of the consumer. This is demonstrated by brain research with the aid of magnetic resonance imaging[3] as well as blind tests with consumers (cf. Fig. 2.2).

Efficient vertical price care is indispensable, not only for cult products like this fizzy drink, but for (almost) all branded articles. Strong brands are created in peoples' minds through their own experiences and beliefs, and these are influenced, firstly, by 'storytelling' in the media and, secondly, and in particular, by personal communication at sales outlets. Discord between manufacturers and sales agents would upset the brand community.

It is generally the case that unbridled price destruction and uncoordinated brand management can damage strong brands or even destroy them.

[3] More information on this in Ahlert and Hubert (2010, pp. 59ff) and Kenning (2010, pp. 31ff).

The legal system does not currently offer any effective protection against these processes. If the individual supplier is then also prohibited from taking action himself to protect his brand against such impairments, he may lose customers. The product pales into insignificance. Diversity and, consequently, welfare, are lost if the consumer is unnecessarily forced to forego consumption. Without strong brands, consumer welfare is diminished.[4] In the case of the cult beverage, Red Bull, some would perhaps say: 'Just as well that we have got rid of this useless beverage. Young people should go back to drinking mineral water, milk or beer.' The market has been cleaned up. In the words of Josef Schumpeter: the brand has been creatively destroyed, space has been created for the invention and marketing of new products. Or, as Friedrich Nietzsche said: '...and he who would be a creator in good and evil—truly he must first be a destroyer and break values.' (Zarathustra 1928).

2.3 How Does Vertically Coordinated Price Management Affect the Dynamics of Innovation in Manufacturing and Retailing?

The above consideration is based on a fatal misunderstanding of industrial processes of innovation in connection with price maintenance. The argument repeatedly raised that price maintenance leads to *lethargy in competition* and diminishes willingness to innovate and the force of innovation in a sector is untenable in its claim of general validity. It can claim validity only in the extreme scenario of insurmountable barriers to market entry (i.e. high protective fences for obsolete products). In the normal case, the *interdependency between vertical price management and the dynamics of innovation* is precisely reversed. What entrepreneur would invest in complex processes of innovation if he expected that his supply concept could not reach the consumer in unadulterated form, because it would be immediately caught up in price wars? Who would invest in innovative supply concepts if the development of a strong brand was doomed to failure from the outset, because of the legal prohibition of concerted practices in the sales channel? All the more so if this led to a situation in which distributors who had been willing to cooperate were to lose interest in the transaction because of inadequate margins and the necessary enthusiasm for storytelling could not even arise.

In order to provide sound answers in terms of the theory of competition to the questions raised above, a brief *excursion into competition as a process of discovery* is required. The processes of progress can be described as the most important subprocesses of effective competition, but also as those most susceptible to disruption.

[4] Cf. the article by Mocken (2012).

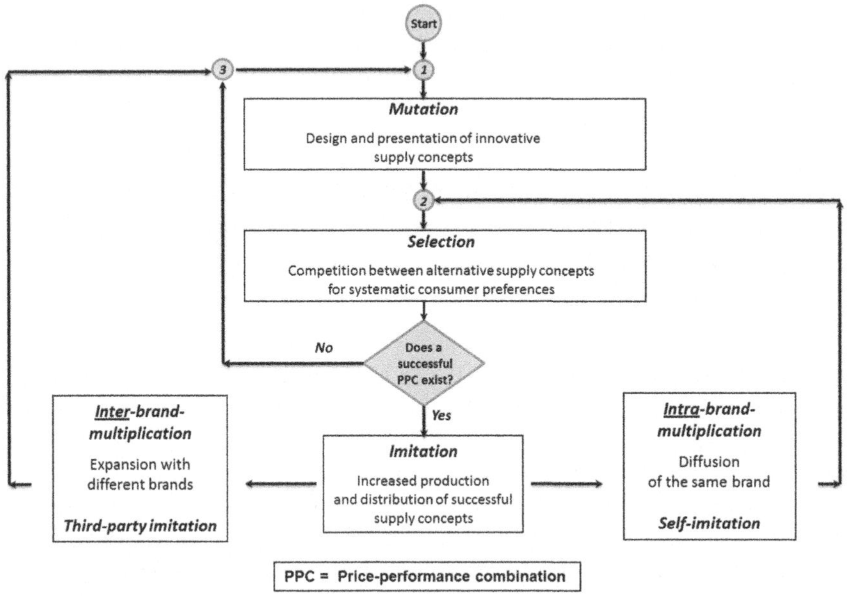

Fig. 2.3 Competition as a process of discovery (following Grossekettler)

According to the economist, Heinz Grossekettler, they can be presented as follows[5]:

Even consumers do not generally know exactly what their preferences will be before new goods emerge. Needs for 'unborn' goods exist latently at best. In this situation, it is important for consumers to be presented with the *widest possible range of alternative problem solutions* (items satisfying needs) in the course of a market experiment. Through their purchasing decisions, consumers determine the chances of survival of the individual supply concepts and, therefore, the possible returns to the supplying companies. This is how *consumer sovereignty* finds expression.

The process of innovation and diffusion is divided schematically into four sub-processes: mutation, selection, self-imitation and third-party imitation (cf. Fig. 2.3). In the consumer-goods sector, innovative supply concepts normally arise through a division of labour by the interaction of manufacturer and distributors (*mutation*). Value systems which prove to have greater than average success, owing to a high degree of consumer acceptance (*selection*) expand by increasing their capacities and consolidating their position with proven means. We refer to this process of *self-imitation* within the value system as *intra*-brand multiplication. Success motivates competing value systems to disseminate 'me-too products' or

[5] Cf. Grossekettler (1981, p. 255ff), (2009, p. 139ff).

even wholly innovative variations of the successful concept under alternative labels (manufacturer brands or trademarks). The process of *third-party imitation* may, therefore, be called *inter-brand* multiplication.

2.4 Why can the Prohibition of Vertical Price and Brand Maintenance Disrupt the Processes of Progress and, Therefore, the Effectiveness of Inter-Brand Competition?

Potential for disruption can be located in all four sub-processes of competition as a process of discovery and they are also closely related to each other. For example, foreseeable future difficulties in the diffusion of an innovative product, possibly based on a lack of cooperation on the part of the trade target group, may negatively affect *industry willingness mutate*. A distributor's lack of will to cooperate may, in turn, be traced back to his experiences with his distributor colleagues within the same value system. Loss-leader offers, confusing signals from sales personnel, inadequate goods presentation etc. can cause *consumers to doubt the quality*, so that the selection process is disrupted. Consequently, no strong brand even develops in the minds of customers (distributors and consumers). Ultimately, the chain reaction of mutually propagating effects that are possible and already foreseeable ex ante discourages manufacturers from investing in complex innovation processes.

This is made clear here again taking the selection process as an example. For the consumer to have any *opportunity of* 'sovereign selection', the supplier (e.g. a branded-article manufacturer) must present his supply concept at all levels in an *unadulterated* manner as far as possible. It would have to be classified as market distortion if brand positioning within the value system intended by the producer was systematically thwarted. This would deny the innovative service opportunity to gain the favour of consumers in the course of the 'market experiment'. Reference is repeatedly made in this context to the risk potential for luxury, prestige or cult goods, but also for high-quality gift articles where, for example, an aggressive low-price policy or loss-leader policy of the distributor or a disharmonious brand communication would run counter to the intended brand launch concept of the manufacturer.

It is the task of competition policy to create suitable underlying conditions that enable innovators to ensure *for themselves* that the supply concepts regarded by them as promising reach the consumer level.

Coordination processes within value systems, explicitly also measures of *vertical brand protection and inter-level price care*, should be admissible in principle, to the extent that they promote the efficient operation of processes of progress. If, on the contrary, an efficient influence by innovators on *intra*-brand multiplication is not legally admissible, there is a risk that no processes of mutation take place, because entrepreneurs assign more importance to the risk of losing the necessary 'return on investment' than to the opportunities associated with innovation. This creates a serious defect in *inter*-brand competition, a deficit which would normally have to be eliminated by competition-policy intervention, but which in fact is caused by the cartel-law regulation of vertical marketing.

Not only the permanent *discovery and diffusion of new products*, but also the stabilisation and, if consumers demonstrate a desire for them by their selection behaviour, possibly also the *expansion of the pre-existing range of services and strong brands* could be the result of competition as a process of discovery. There are close interdependencies between these two processes, the introduction of *new* products and the undistorted marketing of *proven* supply concepts. This is because the *high risk of subsequent brand erosion* can stifle innovation efforts from the outset. Furthermore, the impairment of ongoing business success can prevent the release of investment funds urgently needed for innovation. Such destruction of innovation incentives constitutes *one of the most dangerous distortions of markets.*

2.5 Are Price Reductions a Valid Indicator of Increased Welfare?

The conviction that allowing vertical price coordination would cause higher prices for desired branded goods and that these higher prices would inevitably reduce consumer welfare is apparently widespread in cartel-law practice.[6] In fact, price

[6] Simon (2012) warns urgently against the admissibility of RPM by reference to the *Loi Galland* passed in France: "This is a statute from 1996 whose real purpose was to prohibit major supermarket chains from selling below cost price. Instead the statute operated like price maintenance in the form of minimum prices where suppliers defined high selling prices and granted year-end discounts that were not allowed to influence the retail price. The result of this was a decline in both inter-brand and intra-brand competition. The prices that customers had to pay after the *Loi Galland* were almost 10 % higher in 2002 (1 January 1997 = 100) than in Germany and at least 3 % higher than the average in the remainder of the Eurozone. After it was realized that this statute had negative effects on consumer welfare, it was amended in 2005. Prices fell by four per cent within a period of 14 months."In fact, there is no plausible explanation for the chain of effects 'admissible price restraints ≫ higher price ≫ diminution of consumer welfare'. Because the Loi Galland had a serious defect: it intervened with a further restraint (it imposed a prohibition of less-than-cost price on all participants) in the value chains and, as a result, it stifled effective competition instead of giving back participants their individual freedom of action. If the statute had instead allowed different forms of vertical price coordination, then, with (sufficiently) effective competition, lasting market results would have been seen that would be described as optimum from the point of view of consumer welfare. Should price increases occur as a result of effective

reductions can definitely *not* be regarded as a valid indicator of greater welfare. Welfare is not primarily concerned with—possibly only temporary—price reductions, but instead with the *diverse options facing consumers among various different supply concepts characterised by different prices*. Moreover, the following fact may not be ignored: in the absence of mutation, even the most efficient processes of selection and imitation come to nothing. Destroying incentives to innovate does not lead to cost-effective supplies of attractive products in the long term.

How can a legal system which explicitly allows patents in order to promote innovation, and which has done so for more than 100 years, deny vertical brand protection to an innovative supply concept? If no essential goods are involved, in which case competition policy must naturally prevent extortionate prices, but the free appropriation of income by consumers, the following question arises: why should the State interfere in value processes and limit diversity? This would be according to the motto: 'Unless all consumers can afford to buy expensive cult lemonade, nobody should be allowed to have it.'

References

Ahlert D (2004) Warum ein zentrales Brandcontrolling unverzichtbar wird. In: Markenverband (ed) Ertragsreserven aus Markenkapital, 2nd edition, Wiesbaden, pp 7–28

Ahlert D, Hubert M (2010) Consumer Neuroscience—Anwendung und Nutzen neurowissenschaftlicher Mess-und Analysemethoden in der Konsumentenverhaltensforschung. In: Bruhn M, Köhler R (eds) Wie Marken wirken: Impulse aus der Neuroökonomie für die Markenführung. Munich, pp 59–74

Ahlert D, Kenning P, Plassman H (2006a) Neural correlates of brand choice under uncertainty: The role of brand trust, society for consumer psychology cruise conference

Ahlert D, Kenning P, Plassman H (2006b) A window to the consumer's mind: application of functional brain imaging techniques to advertising research. In: Diehl S, Terlutter R (eds) International advertising and communication—Current insights and empirical findings, Wiesbaden, pp 163–180

Grossekettler H (1981) Die gesamtwirtschaftliche Problematik vertraglicher Vertriebssysteme. In: Ahlert D (ed) Vertragliche Vertriebssysteme zwischen Industrie und Handel, Wiesbaden, pp 255–314

Grossekettler H (2009) Marktprozessbedingte Controllingaufgaben in Unternehmen. In: Schröder H et al (eds) Distribution und Handel in Theorie und Praxis. Festschrift für Prof. Dr. Dieter Ahlert, pp 115–155

Kenning P (2010) Fünf Jahre neuroökonomische Forschung–eine Zwischenbilanz und ein Ausblick. In: Bruhn M, Köhler R (eds) Wie Marken wirken. Impulse aus der Neuroökonomie für die Markenführung, München, pp 31–46

Kenning P, Wobker I (2012) Die negativen Folgen von Kundenverwirrtheit und die moderierende Rolle von Vertrauen in der Konsumgüterdistribution. Konzeptionelles Modell und empirische Befunde. In: Ahlert D, Kenning P, Schröder H, Olbrich R (eds) Vertikale Preis- und Markenpflege im Kreuzfeuer des Kartellrechts, Wiesbaden, pp 69–94

(Footnote 6 continued)
competition—as reasoned in detail in the present article—there would be no doubt as to their economic justification from a welfare point of view (translated from German).

Mocken W (2012) Integrierte Markenführerschaft. Vertriebskooperation zwischen Industrie und Handel. In: Ahlert D, Kenning P, Schröder H, Olbrich R (eds) Vertikale Preis- und Markenpflege im Kreuzfeuer des Kartellrechts, Wiesbaden, pp 227–232

Plassmann H, O'Doherty J, Shiv B, Rangel A (2008) Marketing actions can modulate neural representations of experienced pleasantness. In: PNAS, vol 105, no. 3, pp 1050–1054

Schefer B (2013) Das Verbot der vertikalen Preisbindung, forthcoming

Simon S (2012) Preisbindungen und Preisempfehlungen. Kartellrechtliche Grenzen der vertikalen Kooperation zwischen Industrie und Handel. In: Ahlert D, Kenning P, Schröder H, Olbrich R (eds) Vertikale Preis- und Markenpflege im Kreuzfeuer des Kartellrechts, Wiesbaden, pp 249–256

Zernisch P (2004) Wohin die Ernüchterung aus der Markenmacherei führt, in: Markenverband (ed): Ertragsreserven aus Markenkapital, 2nd edition, Wiesbaden, pp 29–36

Chapter 3
The Risks of Resale Price Maintenance Prohibition for the Effectiveness of Inter-Brand Competition

The conclusion to be drawn from the above statements is that the preservation of supply diversity by protecting strong brands and the expansion of diversity by protecting investments in innovation—given the lack of State protection mechanisms—necessarily requires freedom to take action oneself to regulate internal relationships in value system. However, the *strict prohibition of every form of vertical price and brand care* largely cancels out this freedom. Undisputedly regarded as evident today is the fact that no general increase in welfare is achieved as a result. On the contrary, *the effectiveness of competition between the major brands is seriously endangered.* This evidence is examined once again systematically in this section.

On the other hand, the negative effects on competition of admissible price maintenance assumed again and again are not evident, but can only be concluded purely theoretically. *Not evident* because price restraints (with few exceptions) have long since been prohibited and, therefore, their effects are not observable. According, one can only speculate or theorise as to whether scenarios exist in reality in which the anti-competitive effects of price maintenance, if the latter were admissible, could actually be so great as to outweigh the considerable risks of RPM prohibition. These hypotheses will later be evaluated in Chap. 4.

In the following analysis, the various risks arising from RPM prohibition to competition (and therefore also to consumer welfare) will be divided into five risk levels depending on their severity.

D. Ahlert and B. Schefer, *Vertical Price Coordination and Brand Care*, SpringerBriefs in Business, DOI: 10.1007/978-3-642-35570-7_3,

3.1 Risk Level 1: Preventing Efficiency Advantages of Vertical Price Coordination

As already outlined at the beginning, there is no real need to verify potentially positive effects of admissible price restraints when examining the need for deregulation.[1] Nevertheless, if the risk potential of the RPM prohibition is to be analysed comprehensively, investigating any positive effects of price restraints on competition is unavoidable. This is because, if these positive effects actually exist, it is obvious that a blanket RPM prohibition causes harm, because it systematically prevents the occurrence of these positive effects.

It is extremely difficult to make a complete list of the efficiency advantages. Whether price restraints can in fact have positive effects and, consequently (if legally admissible) establish themselves on the market,[2] depends on their relative advantageousness compared to alternative price-formation processes. This applies equally to contractual partners in the value chain (manufacturers and distributors) as well as and primarily from the perspective of consumers. Price-maintenance systems will not become established in the absence of consumer acceptance. Estimating or even forecasting the specific impact of such agreements on market results with sufficient precision, by the State, by the European Commission or by anyone else, in order to decide on admissibility in individual cases, must be described as a 'pretence of competence'.

In statements on cartel-law practice (e.g. Block Exemption Regulation, Guidelines on Vertical Restraints, statements by the competition authorities), such efficiency advantages are mentioned only for a few obvious cases. For an example, reference is made to the efficiencies that could justify an individual exemption specified in paragraph 225 of the Vertical Guidelines 2010[3]:

- *Market launch of a new product* where the manufacturer can attract distributors for market entry by means of price fixing and these distributors in turn invest in sales-promotion measures.

---

[1] The examination of deregulation serves the purpose of *fundamental* clarification of the law to be made *(de lege ferenda)* of whether a restrictive legal provision has become outdated and, therefore, should be abolished. It cannot be confused with the individual case examination under applicable law (*de lege lata*) (for example, in accordance with Article 101(3) TFEU), by which a company can (subsequently) obtain exemption from a general prohibition by providing detailed evidence for the present *individual case* that there are positive effects that outweigh the anti-competitive effects (cf. Vertical GL, paragraph 5).

[2] Under effective competition, only those vertical restraints become established on the market which bring relative efficiency benefits to the consumer: They have a *right to exist because they exist*. There is no need to prove their positive individual effects in order to justify them.

[3] It seems unnecessary to consider this in more detail at this point, because several articles give this subject detailed consideration. Cf. Blechman (2012), Haucap and Klein (2012), Schwalbe (2012), Simon (2012) and Wey (2012).

- *Short-term special-offer campaigns* (two to six weeks) in franchise systems or similar distribution systems where the greatest possible advertising impact is achieved using uniform low prices.
- *Elimination of the free-rider problem* especially with products requiring detailed advice, where a structure of uniform selling prices enables distributors to continue offering the necessary advisory service, that incurs extra costs.

In numerous academic articles, it has almost become standard to first of all concede the above-mentioned positive effects of price fixing (and a few others[4]) in order then to disqualify them by reference to their (allegedly) harmful effects on horizontal competition.[5] The argument that the RPM prohibition should be abolished, because it prevents the welfare gains on the part of consumers associated with the above effects, is countered with the argument that there is nothing to prevent the participants affected from verifying the pro-competitive and pro-welfare effects of price restraints under the *defence of efficiency under Art. 101 (3) TFEU* and thereby legalising them in individual cases. However, as shown in Sect. 5.3, this construct of the individual exemption is economically flawed. This is because no entrepreneur can seriously afford to get involved in a highly complex, time-consuming and extremely risky defence of efficiency.

3.2 Risk Level 2: Direct Reduction of Diversity Due to Prohibition of Attractive Price-Formation Processes

From a welfare perspective, the effectiveness of competition between different supply concepts (i.e. inter-brand competition) represents the greatest conceivable gain for consumers. Desirable for competition policy reasons is, therefore, a situation in which consumers are able to choose from an abundant range of both similar types of, as well as differently structured supply combinations and accordingly, have plenty of alternative options. A branch of industry can be regarded as diverse, as the most important result of effective competition if, in the totality of the supply concepts offered, an extensive range of the components (type of performance, price-formation processes, brand architecture and organisation type) can be found (see Fig. 3.1). Ultimately, it depends on the diversity demanded

---

[4] In addition to the above-mentioned effects, it is occasionally admitted that the price maintenance can, under certain circumstances, resolve the problem of 'double marginalization' in bilateral monopolies in which case, however, it is necessary to ask whether no more suitable ('less anti-competitive') methods exist. Cf. Schwalbe (2012) and Wey (2012) for more detail.

[5] For example, recital no. 10 of Block Exemption Regulation 2010 states: 'In particular, vertical agreements containing certain types of severe restrictions of competition such as minimum and fixed resale-prices, as well as certain types of territorial protection, should be excluded from the benefit of the block exemption established by this Regulation, irrespective of the market share of the undertakings concerned.'.

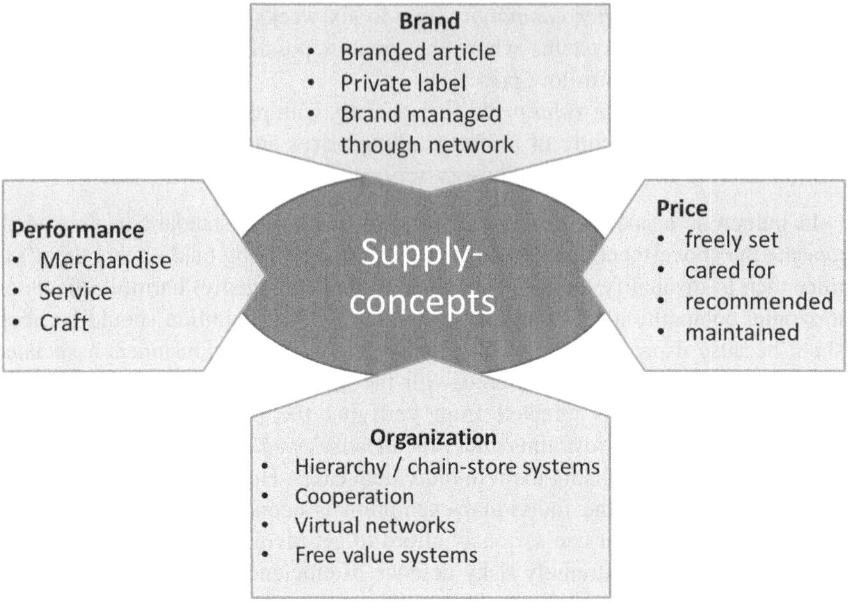

Fig. 3.1 Design elements of complex supply-concepts

by consumers. An artificial restriction of heterogeneity, e.g. through the legal system, leads (almost inevitably) to sub-optimum solutions in terms of welfare.

The call for the most unrestricted diversity of the supply concepts available to the consumer for selection also expressly applies to *freedom of choice in vertical pricing processes.* If the consumer were to be allowed to choose, for example, between price-maintained and non-price-maintained products, this could represent greater 'welfare' than if he were denied this opportunity to choose.

Of major importance is that intensive competition through price-formation processes for the favour of the consumer takes place.

If RPM prohibition were to be abolished, *attractive price-policy heterogeneity* could emerge for the consumer, through consumer-goods distribution processes. Here are just a few examples:

- Some of the supply concepts competing with each other find favour with consumers, because prices change constantly. This may suit those consumers seeking variety or who are on the lookout for bargains. Permanent price variations may be centrally controlled, in which case the branded article manufacturer, or the central office of a retailing system, as is the case for trademarks, can assume the control function. However, price formation can also be left to the free play of market forces within the value chain.

- Many consumers swear by price consistency, either to show appreciation in the case of gifts or because of conspicuous consumption or the snob effect or because they do not wish to be upset by the thought of having paid too high a price. The extensive literature on price management has elaborated numerous other reasons why consumers would prefer price-maintained goods if they were permitted.[6]
- Numerous value systems are characterised by the fact that distributors, as participants 'on the consumer front', at no time want to be deprived of sovereignty over price structuring, even if price restraints were allowed. The price-forming processes here, therefore, focus on distributors.
- Other business models are particularly successful, because of the fact that it is not the local retailer, but the network centre of a cooperative value system or even the manufacturer that operates price management, thereby relieving retailers of the difficult business of price calculation.[7]
- Many distributors place great value on the guidance role of recommended prices, others need no such assistance. For consumers too, recommended prices can be a valuable aid to selection.
- Hierarchically organised systems (e.g. chain-store systems, vertical systems) have always had complete freedom of action in vertical price management, because they are not subject to RPM prohibition. However, this has not necessarily led to central price control or to price consistency. Within the hierarchy, decentralised decision-making has frequently proved economically superior.

We wish to show by these examples the variety of 'customer-oriented solutions' that could emerge from competition as a process of discovery, if it were not restricted by cartel law. The RPM prohibition considerably restricts this range of alternatives, reducing in the consumption options open to the consumer (e.g. prices for 'his' brands that are uniform and/or stable over time). The consumer is forced to resort to second-best solutions. This constitutes a *considerable restriction of competition which is caused by applicable competition law.* It is surprising that this risk potential has not so far been regarded as a problem in the Block Exemption Regulation or the Guidelines or also in the controversial discussion.

---

[6] Cf. for an overview Ahlert (2004) and Ahlert et al. (2006).

[7] In a qualitative survey by the Institute of Retailing and Network Marketing at the University of Muenster, in 2010, many distributors stated that it would be wholly uneconomic for them to calculate every price for the approx. 50,000 articles that they have on offer. For this purpose, they would have to employ several business managers or else immediately petition for insolvency. Moreover, they were completely reliant on the central price labeling by manufacturers on grounds of costs. In hierarchical systems, central price control is permitted; for free and cooperative value systems, this is strictly prohibited. This means that these systems have no alternative but to transform themselves into vertical chain-store systems and, therefore, choose a form of organization that is economically worse from their point of view.

3.3 Risk Level 3: Indirect Reduction of Diversity Due to Prohibition of Efficient Communication and Division-of-Labour Relationships in Value Networks

The numerous regulations from the competition authorities, courts and European Commission in their interpretation of the *unclear legal concepts in the German and European cartel law* can do considerably greater harm to the effectiveness of competition (and, therefore, to consumer welfare) than the RPM prohibition itself. Similar to the fight against horizontal 'hardcore price cartels' where such additional protection (within economically reasonable limits) may be desirable, *many supplementary regulations on practices* have recently been introduced for the vertical relations between manufacturing and retailing. They appear similarly naive in some cases, to a desire to prevent cartels by banning the telephone. The primary purpose of these additional regulations consists of categorically preventing all conceivable attempts to bypass the RPM prohibition. When there are complaints in practice about the considerable collateral damage caused by the RPM prohibition and the growing legal uncertainty, it is largely this tight network of rules that is meant.[8]

Reference is made to just a few examples from the recommendation *(Handreichung)* of the Federal Cartel Office (cf. Annex I). It lists a wealth of practices within value chains as (potentially) inadmissible or at risk of cartel-law purposes, to the extent to which they were connected in any way to vertical price care. The starting point of the recommendation is an axiom evidently regarded as irrefutable in cartel-law [9]:

> Price competition in the trade with consumer goods is characterised by the fact that wholesale and retail companies set their own prices themselves, on the basis of the negotiated manufacturer ex works prices and their own price policies, and themselves bear the economic risk of their price policies.

That sounds as if the control of distributors over ultimate-consumer prices were a *law of nature*. Every measure or arrangement within the value chain which could put this law of nature out of action is classified as an inadmissible restriction of the freedom of action on the part of the trade, even if the distributor displays a lively

[8] As demonstrated by Glowik (2012), from the Unilever company, with impressive examples from the everyday practice of business transactions between the numerous sellers from industry and buyers from retailing, the requirements of cartel-law practice (by competition authorities, courts) outlined in the recommendation (Handreichung) e.g. on communications within the value chain, are largely unrealistic. Whether they wish to or not, participants in the companies are unable to implement them in practice. The requirements derived from the interpretation of non-specific legal concepts of the GWB are not practicable – quite apart from the fact that they must frequently be regarded as not in conformity with the principle from a competition point of view—and, for this reason, they should be cancelled without delay.

[9] Cf. Federal Cartel Office (Bundeskartellamt 2010).

interest in such agreements for reasons of efficiency.[10] The finding frequently also encountered in academic articles that sovereignty over prices lies 'by nature' with the distributor, is not comprehensible in economic terms.[11]

The present-day reality in the consumer-goods sector is such that hierarchical, cooperating and free value systems with differing combinations of risk spreading and decision-making compete for consumers. Manufacturers' brands, trademarks and distributors' brands can have a decisive effect on supply concepts. *Competition between the systems* has given rise to different system heads, as dominant controlling instances within the value systems. Where it is not distributors, but manufacturers or network centres (e.g. franchisors) who act as system heads, it appears naive and absurd for the State to wish to deprive the latter of their authority in the area of price policy, one of the most important marketing tools[12]:

Allowing exclusively *distributor*-controlled price systems represents a radical restriction of diversity and cannot be justified with regard to the competition-policy principle of effective market processes.

Equally questionable in economic terms are *restrictions of the division of labour, specialisation and risk spreading within value systems.* All without exception obstruct market processes of efficient distribution. There should be no interference in division-of-labour structures by the State, merely to keep alive a blanket RPM prohibition for which there is no longer any justification (see Chap. 4) and then do so only unilaterally in the case of free and cooperative value systems (see also Sect. 3.5). To this extent, the criticism of the German HDE retail federation can be supported,[13] which regards the opinion in the above-mentioned axiom as misguided, i.e. that a commercial company must, after concluding negotiations with a branded-article manufacturer on the basis of the negotiated purchase price, bear the entire economic risk for these branded goods itself. Why should an agreement, for example, in which the manufacturer guarantees a distributor a minimum return or minimum margin with his product (similar to the access

---

[10] Sanktjohanser (2012) (HDE) argues in similar manner: 'Agreements on selling prices between commerce and industry must remain in the future, as equally inadmissible as horizontal price agreements. Selling prices must be set autonomously by retailers! Any other solution would be to the detriment of consumers.' As shown by our own empirical surveys, this categorical opinion is not shared by all sectors of the consumer-goods sector and all consumers (translated from German).

[11] Lademann (2012) comes to the same conclusion.

[12] Cf. also the article by Greipl (2012) on this discussion.

[13] Statement of the HDE of 17 August on the provisional evaluation of practices in negotiations between manufacturers of branded articles, wholesalers and retail enterprises by the Federal Cartel Office of 13 April 2010 and the article by Sanktjohanser (2012)

payments for shelf space or promotion space expressly exempted by the EU Commission[14]) not be admissible?

Regarded as particularly serious are tendencies in cartel-law practice which lead to a de facto situation of imposing a *far-reaching prohibition on communication and cooperation on value systems* that are not organised hierarchically. At least this is perceived as such in many cases by companies (and their legal advisers) with regard to the operative exchange of information. This also applies to the strategic coordination[15] of market-launch concepts, in brand communications and in the case of cooperative category management.[16] Since 'value partners' can never be quite certain as to whether a link with cartels or vertical price agreements could be construed or brought about by definition[17] in the vertical exchange of information or their cooperation projects, the current inclination is to completely abstain from such modes of conduct as a precaution. This can lead to an economically questionable chain reaction whose consequences may be inefficiencies, an impoverishment of the commercial landscape and, therefore, the stifling of diversity.[18]

Recent trends towards expanding the dense network of regulations cannot be disregarded as negligible. In our view, they contain one of the greatest potential current risks to the consumer-goods sector.

The *observable consequences of legal uncertainty* are serious: numerous companies had abandoned their practice-proven inter-level cooperation projects such as vertical category management in 2010, because of (real or possibly imaginary) threats from cartel law. This is highly regrettable from a marketing point of view because such joint concepts of manufacturing and retailing have met with substantial consumer acceptance.[19] Moreover, the necessary coordination of brand strategy in the value chain is increasingly being abandoned, e.g. about the target positioning of the branded article and shopping locations, because they

[14] Cf. Vertical GL, paragraph 207f.

[15] Cf. the definition of coordination in Section II of the recommendation ('Handreichung'): 'Concerted practices as distinguished from contractual agreement lie in every form of communication that does not lead to the conclusion of a contract, but which deliberately allows practical cooperation to take the place of the competition associated with risk. This practical cooperation creates competition conditions that do not correspond to normal market conditions.' From an economic perspective, it cannot be said what normal market conditions are. Practical cooperation in value chains has tended to be the rule rather than the exception until now; prohibiting such cooperation cannot necessarily be regarded as intervention in conformity with the principle (translated from German).

[16] See Schröder (2012) for more details.

[17] Cf. also the pertinent notes by Glowik (2012) (Unilever) on the problem of being muzzled in everyday business of employees in the sales and purchasing departments.

[18] Cf. also the urgent appeal by Greipl (2012).

[19] Cf. also the detailed article by Schröder (2012).

could become connected with elements of a concerted price structure (and could, therefore, potentially lead to legal proceedings). Owing to the considerable personal risks involved, managers in particular are no longer prepared to venture into such experiments in vertical marketing.

3.4 Risk Level 4: Prevention of Diversity by Stifling Innovation and Impairing Strong Brands

The *disruption of innovative processes* can be regarded as the *most serious form of market failure* caused mainly by RPM prohibition. To avoid repetition, we refer to the arguments in Chap. 2. The interdependencies between the impairment of strong brands and the dynamics of innovation are also outlined.

It is necessary to consider the following additional aspects at this point. Following the recent tightening up of the 'extended RMP prohibition complex' outlined above, there is almost no action whatsoever that value partners can take themselves to combat *flagrant excesses of intra-brand price wars as far as brand erosion*. It is not only branded articles with sensitive images that suffer, but also the shop images of numerous distributors who cannot credibly enter the market with extremely low prices—and, because of the prohibition on prices below cost-prices (sec. 20 (4) GWB), they are possibly not allowed to do so.[20] From the perspective of the branded-goods industry, however, consideration is given not merely to selling below cost price, but also to other forms of low-price offers (e.g. loss leaders or tie-in offers) and value-destroying market practices also referred to as 'price destruction' or 'selling at crash prices'. These practices are not only damaging to the quality perception of the branded article, but also reduce the utility of items of prestige, or products intended to impress guests or donees.[21] Above all, however, consideration must be given to the lasting reduction of consumer willingness to pay the prevailing price, even if the price reduction represents merely a temporary phenomenon. Not necessarily immediately, but usually after a time, *the classic branded article loses its confidence function* as a consequence of low-price strategies or other derogatory activities within the value system and this raises complexity for the consumers. This has fatal consequences for strong brands which define themselves by guiding decision-making.[22]

---

[20] It is mentioned in passing that this prohibiting provision proves to be a blunt tool of cartel law, as shown by the recent decision of the Federal Court of Justice in the case of the drugstore operator Rossmann. The authority's order imposing a fine on Rossmann had to be cancelled. Nevertheless, it does not appear sensible to conclude from this that the prohibiting provision must be made even stricter. On the contrary, this legal provision, like all other regulations of intra-brand competition, is highly questionable in principle: It is not stricter regulations that are required; instead deregulation of consumer-goods distribution is long overdue!

[21] Cf. also the comprehensive article by Greipl (2012).

[22] Cf. also the detailed article by Kenning and Wobker (2012).

From the perspective of specialist distributors, the risk potential of intra-brand price wars is such that even if their sales policy focuses on the quality of their listed articles and the services provided, specialist distributors are equally reliant on consumers regarding the prices as fair—a fact that is frequently overlooked. Those who purchase quality especially, moreover, those in the 'luxury segment' are often careful to ensure that they are not exploited in terms of price by suppliers (manufacturers and distributors). Low-price sales of branded articles, offered shortly beforehand at the 'normal price' or still being offered at the normal price in other shops at the same time, create an *almost irremediable impression of being ripped off.* The consumer may regard as responsible for this misconduct, not just the distributor offering at the higher price, but also the manufacturer whom the consumer may blame for price discrimination to their disadvantage. If the specialist retailer is not in a position immediately to match the low price of an aggressive price competitor or to immediately remove the product from the list, this may revive the *deep-rooted* 'preconception of price extortion', in Germany sometimes called as *Apothekenpreis-Vorurteil.* A significant price difference for just one staple article in the product range of the specialist distributor compared to a competitor may cause the consumer to think: *I always knew that they were too expensive.* In the food sector, not only 'delicatessens' suffer from this preconception, but also independent food traders who can be considered full-range suppliers among the 'specialist distributors of this sector', no matter how favourably priced they offer their price-entry selection.

Not least, recent qualitative research by the Institute of Retailing and Network Marketing at the University of Muenster shows that RPM prohibition prevents middle-class enterprises from the superior power of other parties in negotiations.[23] For example, specialist distributors take advantage of the potential to discuss retail prices, specifically problems arising from increases in ex-work prices. On the other hand, communication about retail prices often helps well-known middle-class manufacturers, who are popular with consumers, to avoid losses resulting from renegotiations with superior distributors at the end of the year.

Precautions in the form of vertical price and brand care may be necessary and should thus be admissible, so that incentives to develop and establish innovative products and develop strong brands are not destroyed.

One of the major causes of disruptions to innovation is the RPM prohibition complex (increasingly exacerbated by supplementary directives) which prohibits market operators from taking action themselves to prevent the stifling of innovation and the impairment of their brands in the value chain.

[23] See for this and thereafter Schefer (2013) (forthcoming).

3.5 Risk Level 5: Structural Distortion Through Unequal Legal Treatment of Competing Types of Organisations

Competition policy repeatedly considers, for consumer-goods sectors undergoing strong transformation, whether distribution already has an *optimum structure from the consumer perspective*. If not, this would constitute a shortcoming. This leads to the next question of whether the State can influence the structural development of consumer-goods distribution in such a way as to improve consumer welfare, as demonstrated by better market results (sustained diversity of supply with attractive products at favourable prices). With a view fostering effective competition, the answer to this question must be *no*. The mechanisms giving rise to diversity, in this case, the distribution landscape, are so complex that it would be equivalent to a 'pretence at knowledge' (v. Hayek) for the State to diagnose, forecast or even optimise it. It is not even possible to answer the first question. Since no one really knows what constitutes optimum economic structures, no one can assess whether or not they prevail from a consumer perspective.

The only way in which the State can contribute towards optimising distribution is to protect the effectiveness of market processes. Any attempt, no matter how well intentioned, to intervene in vertical distribution structures, directly or indirectly, leads to a sub-optimum result, in comparison to the free play of forces. Provided that the effectiveness of the markets is assured, consumers experience the exact commercial and distribution landscape that they have sovereignly elected. Loosely based on John Richard Hicks, one could also say:

A given distribution structure has the right to exist because it exists!

In fact, the State does not practise any abstention whatsoever, when it comes to influencing distribution structures. An initial example of State intervention, contrary to the guiding principle, was already mentioned in Sect. 3.3. It entails the *increasingly strict regulation of the division of labour, specialisation and spread of risks within value systems*, as added support for RPM prohibition. Nevertheless, the retention of RPM prohibition presents an even greater potential risk to the extent to which there is *discrimination against some competing types of organisation* within the value systems.

The inequality of treatment under cartel law primarily causes a systematic distortion of competition between value systems of hierarchical organisation and those without hierarchical control.

The RPM prohibition operates selectively and therefore distorts structures. It restricts freedom of action in cooperatively organised forms of distribution without hierarchies, but not in value systems controlled by hierarchies. The latter include individual companies and corporations operating over several levels (e.g. chain-store systems for consumer goods) and the vertical systems, which at least partially integrate production and distribution levels (with regard to specific merchandise groups). In this context it is possible to distinguish between forward integration (e.g. shop concepts) and backward integration (e.g. trademark concepts). Hierarchical forms of organisation are generally permitted to do everything that cooperating and free distribution systems are currently strictly prohibited from doing, for example, multi-level price management. What is noticeable is the fact that trademark management within chain-store systems is also not subject to RPM prohibition, although this is the case for cooperative confederations in retailing. Finally the branded-article industry that does not integrate several levels is almost completely denied vertical brand protection.[24]

It cannot be stated too often that any cartel-law interference with the freedom of action within the value chain must satisfy strict criteria for its justification. In case of doubt, such interference must be rejected as breaching the guiding principle. All in all, the further development of consumer-goods distribution is determined to a great extent by legal intervention. Greater verticalisation will occur, combined with questionable welfare effects, to the extent that freedom of contract is reduced in free and cooperative value systems. From a consumer point of view, there is no objection in principle to multi-level verticalisation. Attractive value systems such as IKEA, ZARA, H and M were created by this means and have considerably enriched the range of diversity. However, if this development is accompanied by a *systematic cartel-law impairment of free and cooperative value systems*, it is likely that legally privileged supply concepts will become more established than supply concepts that are more attractive (more efficient) from the consumer point of view.

3.6 Conclusion on the Risk Potential of Resale Price Maintenance Prohibition

The arguments of supporters of the price-maintenance prohibition (cf. Chap. 4) frequently ignore the substantial risks to the effectiveness of competition, such as those arising from cartel-law intervention in the freedom of action of the value systems. An overview of this problem is given in Fig. 3.2. The retention of RPM prohibition, therefore, has huge negative effects on competition and welfare and it

[24] Cf. also the detailed article by Olbrich and Grewe (2012) on this risk potential of the RPM prohibition.

Effects on welfare and competition of state intervention into the freedom of price formation within the value chain

- Preventing efficency advantages of admissible price restraints for the consumer, although legally recognized in the Guidelines on Vertical Restraints (in view of the flaws in the Guidelines for individual exemptions)
- Direct reduction of diversity due to prohibition of price-formation processes that are attractive to consumers (e.g. temporally stable, unitary minimum prices for all consumers)
- Prevention of distribution optimization through indirect reduction of diversity due to prohibition of efficient communication and division-of- labour relationships in value networks
- Reduction of diversity through destruction of strong brands, destruction of innovation incentives and dangers to interactive innovation processes
- Structural distortion through unequal legal treatment of competing types of organisations

Fig. 3.2 Negative effects on welfare and competition of RPM prohibition

is necessary to clarify whether the cumulated risk potential of RPM prohibition shown here can be outweighed by the potentially negative effects of price restraints, if they were allowed.

References

Ahlert D (2004) Gehört das Preisbindungsverbot abgeschafft? Eine disziplinübergreifende Betrachtung auf der Basis des Koordinationsmängel-Diagnose-Konzepts. In: Milbradt G, Deubel I (eds) Ordnungspolitische Beiträge zur Finanz- und Wirtschaftspolitik, Berlin, pp 241–262

Ahlert D, Köster L, Vering S (2006) Preisbindungsverbot auf dem Prüfstand. In: Prießnitz H (ed) Markenführung im Billigzeitalter, Wertevernichtung—Spirale ohne Ende, Landsberg am Lech, pp 211–227

Blechman M (2012) Unreasonable Restraints of Trade Die Entwicklung der Rechtsprechung zum Preisbindungsverbot in den USA. In: Ahlert D, Kenning P, Schröder H, Olbrich R (eds) Vertikale Preis- und Markenpflege im Kreuzfeuer des Kartellrechts, Wiesbaden, pp 199–204

Federal Cartel Office (Bundeskartellamt) (13 April 2010) Betr.: Ordnungswidrigkeitenverfahren wegen des Verdachts vertikaler Preisbindung zwischen Markenartikelherstellern von Süßwaren, Tiernahrung und Kaffee und Unternehmen des Lebensmitteleinzelhandels sowie wegen des Verdachts der mittelbaren Abstimmung von Endverbraucherpreisen zwischen Unternehmen des Lebensmitteleinzelhandels; hier: Vorläufige Bewertung von Verhaltensweisen in Verhandlungen zwischen Herstellern von Markenartikeln, Großhändlern und

Einzelhandelsunternehmen zum Zwecke der Konkretisierung der Kooperationspflichten, Bonn

Glowik J (2012) Das große Schweigen—oder dient ein offener Diskurs zwischen Handel und Industrie den Interessen der Verbraucher? Einige Denkanstöße aus der Praxis In: Ahlert D, Kenning P, Schröder H, Olbrich R (eds) Vertikale Preis- und Markenpflege im Kreuzfeuer des Kartellrechts, Wiesbaden, pp 243–248

Greipl E (2012) Retail Brand-Politik. Die Funktion des Markenartikels. In: Ahlert D, Kenning P, Schröder H, Olbrich R (eds) Vertikale Preis- und Markenpflege im Kreuzfeuer des Kartellrechts, Wiesbaden, pp 211–220

Haucap J, Klein G (2012) Einschränkungen der Preisgestaltung im Einzelhandel aus wettbewerbsökonomischer Perspektive. In: Ahlert D, Kenning P, Schröder H, Olbrich R (eds) Vertikale Preis- und Markenpflege im Kreuzfeuer des Kartellrechts, Wiesbaden, pp 169–186

Lademann RP (2012) Die ökonomischen Aspekte der Preisempfehlung im Lichte von Besonderheiten der Ernährungswirtschaft. In: Ahlert D, Kenning P, Schröder H, Olbrich R (eds) Vertikale Preis- und Markenpflege im Kreuzfeuer des Kartellrechts, Wiesbaden, pp 233–242

Kenning P, Wobker I (2012) Die negativen Folgen von Kundenverwirrtheit und die moderierende Rolle von Vertrauen in der Konsumgüterdistribution. Konzeptionelles Modell und empirische Befunde. In: Ahlert D, Kenning P, Schröder H, Olbrich R (eds) Vertikale Preis-und Markenpflege im Kreuzfeuer des Kartellrechts, Wiesbaden, pp 69–94

Olbrich R, Grewe G (2012) Vertikale Vertriebssysteme und rechtliche Regulierung der vertikalen Preispflege in Europa. Zu den Begründungszusammenhängen, zur Ungleichbehandlung der Systeme und zu den Konsequenzen für den Konsumgütersektor. In: Ahlert D, Kenning P, Schröder H, Olbrich R (eds) Vertikale Preis- und Markenpflege im Kreuzfeuer des Kartellrechts, Wiesbaden, pp 95–126

Sanktjohanser J (2012) Kooperation zwischen Industrie und Handel. Eine Stellungnahme des HDE zur Handreichung des Bundeskartellamtes. In Ahlert D, Kenning P, Schröder H, Olbrich R (eds) Vertikale Preis- und Markenpflege im Kreuzfeuer des Kartellrechts, Wiesbaden, pp 205–210

Schefer B (2013) Das Verbot der vertikalen Preisbindung, forthcoming

Schröder H (2012) Category Management in der Gruppenfreistellungsverordnung 2010—eine Gefahr für die cooperative Markenführung. In: Ahlert D, Kenning P, Schröder H, Olbrich R (eds) Vertikale Preis- und Markenpflege im Kreuzfeuer des Kartellrechts, Wiesbaden, pp 127–154

Schwalbe U (2012) Wettbewerbsökonomische Aspekte der Preisbindung in Wertschöpfungsketten. In: Ahlert D, Kenning P, Schröder H, Olbrich R (eds) Vertikale Preis- und Markenpflege im Kreuzfeuer des Kartellrechts, Wiesbaden, pp 155–168

Simon S (2012) Preisbindungen und Preisempfehlungen. Kartellrechtliche Grenzen der vertikalen Kooperation zwischen Industrie und Handel. In: Ahlert D, Kenning P, Schröder H, Olbrich R (eds) Vertikale Preis- und Markenpflege im Kreuzfeuer des Kartellrechts, Wiesbaden, pp 249–256

Wey C (2012) Preisempfehlungen aus wettbewerbsökonomischer Sicht. In: Ahlert D, Kenning P, Schröder H, Olbrich R (eds) Vertikale Preis- und Markenpflege im Kreuzfeuer des Kartellrechts, Wiesbaden, pp 221–226

Chapter 4
The Risks of Admissible Price-Maintenance Systems for the Effectiveness of Inter-Brand Competition

'It is no longer disputed that vertical restraints may have positive competition-policy effects. The negative effects of vertical price restraints are, on the other hand, much more difficult to determine.'[1] This situation is partly due to the fact that almost no experience with the effect of price maintenance is available, as it has been prohibited in Germany since 1973 (apart from some exceptions). Therefore, one can only speculate or theorise on the impact.

4.1 Price Restraints in the Conflict Between Intra-Brand and Inter-Brand Competition

Vertical price-maintenance systems *primarily* affect behavioural relationships *within* value chains. Nevertheless, the opinion of many economists is as follows: *Price maintenance quite obviously eliminates intra-brand competition—which is definitely harmful to competition!*[2]

First of all, it is not clear what exactly is meant, whether this assumed effect relates solely to competition on *prices* or also to competition with respect to *performance*. However, assuming that competition within one and the same brand would actually be impaired on balance, what would be the appropriate competition-policy consequences? This requires a fundamental clarification of whether competition between several distributors who compete for the same consumers within one and the same value system (i.e. *intra-brand competition*), is even protected by the German Act against Restraints of Competition (GWB). There is no express mention thereof in the statute and this raises the following more compelling questions:

- Do consumers have a 'natural' right to intensive *intra*-brand competition?
- Does intense price competition within one and the same brand have any advantage whatsoever for consumer welfare or is even indispensable to it?

[1] Möschel in his speech at the symposium on 27 January 2011 in Münster (translated from German).
[2] Wey in his speech at the symposium on 20 January 2011 in Bonn (translated from German).

D. Ahlert and B. Schefer, *Vertical Price Coordination and Brand Care*, SpringerBriefs in Business, DOI: 10.1007/978-3-642-35570-7_4,

- Is the attempt by a branded-article manufacturer to harness internal competition within his value system equivalent to a relevant competitive restraint?

Given the pertinent competition-policy principles, these questions cannot be answered affirmatively. Prevailing opinion can be interpreted more as that it is primarily a matter of the *effectiveness of inter-brand competition.* As already discussed, price wars involving the same brand may even be detrimental to consumer welfare. A restriction of competitive relations within value systems through vertical restraints may, depending on the circumstances, be necessary for attractive supply alternatives to be created in the first place and launched in the market, thereby stimulating inter-brand competition. For this reason, the current price-maintenance discussion focuses attention not on the primary, but mainly on the *secondary* effects of price-maintenance systems.[3] It is a question of whether price maintenance can also exclude inter-brand competition or at least impair horizontal competition between the brands. The most common arguments of supporters of strict RPM prohibition are critically examined below, by illuminating the potentially negative effects of price-maintenance systems on competition. Account must always be taken of the fact that several forms of *vertical price and brand care* do not lead to any inflexible and uniform ultimate-consumer prices, so that the negative effects outlined below (e.g. by the support of horizontal price cartels at level of manufacturer and/or distributor) could be omitted from the analysis.

4.2 Effects of Vertical Price Restraints on the Development and Stabilisation of Horizontal Price Cartels

There is general consensus in the literature that vertical price management between manufacturing and retailing in the *extreme form of inflexible fixed-price maintenance* is, under specific circumstances, capable of promoting the formation of horizontal price cartels at the level of distributor and/or manufacturer.[4] The question is, what circumstances enable this to occur? A (fictitious) scenario:

> Imagine a market in which urgently needed essential goods are traded, i.e. staple foods, medicines, drugs and fuels. For this reason, consumers cannot avoid this market by abstention. The market is dominated by a tight oligopoly of suppliers with great market power, is completely stagnant, barely innovative and there are insurmountable barriers to entry. And one now also imagines that almost all manufacturers in this product category have introduced an inflexible fixed-price maintenance system, so that uniform prices for each branded product are charged in all shops in the industry.

---

[3] Cf. on this issue the articles by Blechman (2012), Haucap and Klein (2012), Möschel (2012), Simon (2012), Schwalbe (2012) and Wey (2012).

[4] Cf. as examples Horst (1992, pp. 226ff), Angland (2008, pp. 32f), Bennett et al. (2010, pp. 20ff), Mathewson and Winter (1998, pp. 65ff), Rey and Vergé (2008, pp. 27ff) and the Vertical GL, paragraph 224.

Subject to market principles, such circumstances could justifiably be referred to as a *nightmare scenario*. Anyone who takes this argument as a fundamental starting point is likely to find it difficult, at first glance, to find anything positive about vertical price coordination in the value chain. Nevertheless, it is questionable whether serious accusations have been made at on this basis for the purpose of stifling any critical examination of RPM prohibition from the outset. One could also refer to it as a taboo subject that has influenced the price-maintenance debate for more than 40 years. Above all, the possibility is ignored that the 'nightmare scenario' outlined above could also be the *result of the prohibition of any form of vertical price coordination* whatsoever, and that allowing greater freedom of action could break down market-entry barriers. Moreover, the following questions are worthy of examination:

1. Apart from very few exceptions such as the mineral-oil sector,[5] does this scenario *currently occur* in the current consumer-goods sector?
2. If such isolated, wholly stagnant markets were actually to exist, would it be necessary to use competition policy to counter the *causes*, these being primarily the insurmountable barriers to market entry? Can the imposition of an RPM prohibition be regarded as merely treating the *symptoms*?
3. Even if price restraints could be interpreted as one of the major causal factors of market failure in a few isolated cases, would it not then suffice to limit prohibition to just these cases (*case-by-case approach*)? Conceivable, for example, is an RPM prohibition only for companies dominating the market (a prohibition which already existed prior to 1973) or a limitation of the prohibition to inflexible, undifferentiated fixed-price maintenance systems or to markets with a market share of price-maintained products of, for instance, more than 50 % or a similarly differentiating course of action.

If the inflexible resale fixed-price maintenance were actually to facilitate cartelised structures or even give rise to them this would constitute a strong argument in favour of price-maintenance prohibition. For this reason, the series of arguments used in the literature are presented briefly below.

4.2.1 Vertical Price Maintenance Facilitates Collusion at the Manufacturer Level

A functioning cartel presupposes a prior agreement on promotion parameters (normally prices and quantities) and the monitoring of adherence to them. For this reason, particularly governed by cartel control are the ex-works prices of the

[5] In this sector, the price-maintenance prohibition does not take effect, because suppliers take refuge in agency situations: An eloquent example of the unequal legal treatment of the various forms of organization in consumer-goods distribution.

individual companies and, if appropriate, naturally the fixed retail prices. If final prices are the main subject of the conspiratorial agreement, they are easily monitored, because of the market transparency resulting from price maintenance and, therefore, breaches of cartel agreements are especially easy to uncover.[6] This makes it very clear that *only inflexible fixed-price maintenance systems that are binding on all buyers* can have this effect of easing monitoring. Moreover, the effects are only conceivable in tight oligopolies with high market-entry barriers or even bilateral monopolies, i.e. only in distorted markets.

Angland, Jullien/Rey, Matthewson and Winter and Tesler offer a theoretical explanation for the emergence and stability of a manufacturers' cartel, in terms of ex-works prices on the basis of resale price maintenance.[7] In a world with price-maintenance prohibition, no adherence to the agreed ex-works prices could be observed, because of the bilateral, non-public contractual relations between manufacturing and retailing. Retail prices would be out of the question as a monitoring tool for the efficiency of concerted practices. They would depend not (only) on the agreed ex-works prices of manufacturers, but also be determined by the different, constantly changing cost structures of distributors and numerous uncontrollable environmental influences. As a result, individual members of the cartel could increase their sales through individual price reductions, without being threatened by sanctions for breaching the cartel agreements. By applying a maintained selling price, on the other hand, there would no longer be any incentive for producing companies to generate market shares by means of price discounts in negotiations with distributors; they would have a favourable effect on the distributor's margin only. The stability of the manufacturers' cartel would increase.

In the run-up to the price-maintenance prohibition in Germany in 1973, the federal government argued in a slightly different manner, but with the same result. Since price-maintenance systems prevented distributors from adjusting prices to changed market conditions, they could safeguard their own business operations only in the form of more favourable terms or higher discounts from manufacturers. The industry could respond to this pressure from retail level in the form of a horizontal agreement on terms and conditions and discounts.[8] McLaughlin confirmed the hypothesis that price maintenance encourages collusive behaviour, at least for a specific manufacturers' cartel, 'Bakers of Washington Association'. According to his analysis, this association of various manufacturers of bakery products used vertical price maintenance to enforce agreed market prices.[9]

---

6 Cf. Vertical GL, paragraph 224.

7 Cf. Angland (2008, p. 29), Jullien and Rey (2007), Mathewson and Winter (1998, p. 65) and Telser (1960), cf. also Vertical GL, paragraph 224.

8 Cf. German Bundestag (1962, p. 25).

9 Cf. McLaughlin (1979).

4.2.2 Vertical Price Maintenance Facilitates Collusion at the Distributor Level Within the Framework of Interconnected Hub-and-Spoke Cartels

Collusive behaviour can also occur at the retail level with the aid of price-maintenance mechanisms.[10] In this case, a manufacturer who supplies all distributors, sworn to the conspiracy (a so-called 'common agent') acts as aid to enforce the cartel agreements. He sets a selling price above the free market price, checks any deviations from the agreed equivalent and, if necessary, punishes any "saboteurs".[11] This facilitates the centrally organised set-up and monitoring of cartel structures, regarded as the fundamental problem areas of cartel formation.[12] In this connection, there is frequent mention of star-shaped, hub-and-spoke or 'A to B to C' coordination. Such a situation is conceivable, particularly in the case of well-organised distributors with market power. After all, it would be necessary to 'persuade' the common agent (manufacturer) to pursue such a course of action in the run up. It is assumed in the Guidelines on Vertical Restraints of the European Commission of 19 May 2010, because of the concentration of the horizontal interests of participants who are already strong in the market, that the restrictions (restraints) are ultimately particularly problematic for the consumer.[13]

Here too, it becomes clear that *only inflexible fixed-price maintenance systems binding on all buyers* can have this effect of easier monitoring. Moreover, the effects are only conceivable in situations involving *participants who control the market.*

4.3 Impact of Vertical Price Restraints on the Effectiveness of Competitive Processes

It is not the structures and results of a specific market, but the effectiveness of the competition *processes* that represent the crux of a principle-oriented analysis. Horizontal price cartels, regardless of whether they are at the distributor or manufacturer level, can be regarded as causing the greatest possible impairment to competitive processes. The minimum requirements of functioning markets, i.e. the undistorted operation of market-clearing, profit-normalising, superpower-eroding, product-progress and procedural-progress processes are then no longer met.[14] It is

---

[10] See for this and thereafter Bennett et al. (2010, p. 21) and Mathewson and Winter (1998, pp. 65ff).

[11] It is also possible vice versa that a retailer acts as 'common agent' and enforces a manufacturers' cartel. See also Bernheim and Whinston (1985).

[12] Cf. on this thereafter Lambert (2009, pp. 1944).

[13] Cf. Vertical GL, paragraph 224.

[14] Cf. on this topic Borchert and Grossekettler (1985, pp. 195ff), Grossekettler (1991, p. 467ff), (2009, pp. 175ff).

possible to identify the following negative impairments of competitive processes, based on pre-existing cartel agreements (and, therefore, *possibly* also based on vertical price restraints).[15]

Market-clearance process: The quantity supplied and demanded can no longer be brought to equilibrium by means of price variation, because the market price mechanism is disabled by concerted practices. In the case of inflexible fixed-price maintenance systems that are uniform for all buyers, prices change only rarely, and in leaps and bounds, because they are modified by all suppliers to the same extent, within a narrow time frame.

Return-normalisation process: Cartels are created specifically for the purpose of procuring cartel rents and excess returns, which disable an efficient return-normalisation process. Conceivable consequences are irregularities in production capacities, because the capacity build-up is normally too high and the capacity reduction on the other hand, is too low.

Superpower-erosion process: The concentration on cartelised markets normally lies outside a tolerable range, so that power-building trends are noticeable, which prevent effective variations in structure through market entries.

Product and procedural progress process: Horizontal hardcore price cartels can have negative effects on the innovative force of an economy because, given weakened competition, the need for innovative efforts no longer exists or is greatly lessened. Also, borderline businesses do not leave the market, thereby leading to lethargy in research and development.

The forms of impairment of competition processes listed above refer explicitly to the *pre-existence of cartel agreements*. For this reason, they may be quoted to oppose the admissibility of price-maintenance systems only in the very rare cases in which price maintenance can be revealed as the *cause or stabilising factor* of cartel formation. This in turn applies solely to the extreme form of inflexible fixed-price maintenance systems.

4.4 Effects of Vertical Price Restraints on the Innovativeness of Retailing and Manufacturing Enterprises

Fixed consumer prices are suspected of having a protective effect on less efficient commercial enterprises. Although new and more efficient competitors entering the market could command higher margins and therefore, earn higher profits, they could not exploit the advantages gained from an improved cost structure by reducing prices. Accordingly, there is a competition-diminishing and structure-

[15] Cf. Lorenz (2006), S. 292ff.

distorting effect noted that could cause numerous distributors to initiate resale price maintenance within the distribution system.[16]

This classic arguments originating from the 1960s already had *feet of clay* then and, given the developments in retailing which have meanwhile taken place, have them all the more so today. First of all, it is necessary to draw attention to the fact once again that—if at all—only inflexible fixed-price maintenance systems uniform for all buyers could have this effect and, in turn, could only do so *if all, or at least the most important competing products, were price-maintained.* Obviously overlooked is the fact that the *admissibility of price restraints does not create any obligation to introduce price-maintenance systems*. For the efficient distributors dominant today, *many opportunities* arise, in particular as a result of trademark programmes, *to fight back against price-maintained product sectors*. Moreover, it has repeatedly been shown that a contamination of branches by price-maintenance systems *encourages innovative manufacturers*, not least from other countries and possibly also in cooperation with efficient distributors, to *break down the protecting wall* for weak suppliers on the basis of favourable cost items (cost leadership). As shown below, it must be regarded as highly unlikely that vertical price-maintenance systems could achieve and retain a market share of more than 30 % or even 50 % in any sector. Otherwise, it is clearly the *prohibition* of vertical price and brand maintenance that destroys incentives to innovate, and not the *admissibility* of price restraints.

4.5 Effects of Vertical Price Restraints on Consumer Welfare

Most supporters of prohibition place great emphasis on the hypothesis that price restraints reduce welfare. These vertical restraints are thus attributed considerable potential for the worsening of market results. Negative effects of price restraints have been assumed for the *quantitative market impact* (higher price level, lower quantities) for more than 40 years. However, it is surprising that price maintenance has recently also been blamed for reducing supply diversity (*qualitative market results*).

4.5.1 Vertical Price Maintenance Allegedly Reduces Supply Diversity

The starting point for this proposition is that distorted competition could result from the ability of producing companies to significantly influence trade margins by

[16] Cf. German Bundestag (1962, p. 27) and Vertical GL, paragraph 224. Regarding RPM as a means to soften retail competition also cf. Shaffer (1991).

means of vertical price maintenance.[17] Producers, whose brands are indispensable for a distributor's range of goods, because of their 'radiating effect', could expect that the distributor, in return for adequate margins safeguarded by fixed consumer prices, would be prepared to discriminate against competing products, either by reducing advertising, the standard of service or even by removing the competing products from the range on offer. The effect of this would be to limit the scope of action for (potential) competitors to less attractive distribution platforms or even sales channels. If this argument were to apply, considerable negative effects on the effectiveness of the market, from the process perspective, would also be evident[18]:

Market-clearance and return-normalisation process: The preference of distributors for price-maintained branded articles could deliberately mislead consumers, because they are unaware of the agreements made in the background and would instead assume fair competition between the supply concepts. Consequently, the market clearing process, which brings supply and demand into equilibrium, and the return-normalisation process, which channels production capacities in the direction of demand, could be distorted.

Product and procedural progress process: The likely ultimate consequence would be a reduction in brand diversity, because disadvantaged products could no longer earn the necessary profits and, therefore, would no longer be offered. Potential competitors of the discriminating companies may no longer be able to amortise their investments in research and development. Cost-intensive innovation efforts would be abandoned and incentives to innovation and competition between innovations would be diminished.

This line of argument can be regarded as particularly relevant. It stands and falls with the opportunities (and desire) of distributors to mislead consumers as to the quality of strongly branded products and generally raises the question of whether customer brand loyalty constitutes a barrier to market entry.[19] Interestingly enough, this argument would only be plausible if no more than a small number of the competing products were price-maintained. If, on the other hand, all important branded products were price-maintained, a unilateral preference in retailing could not be blamed for price maintenance. As frequently outlined in the present article, further consideration must be given to the fact that restraining freedom of action (in particular by the prohibition of price maintenance) can also have considerable negative effects on market processes—uncontrolled price wars and brand vandalism can also mislead consumers, destroy incentives to innovate and prevent market entry. In this area of argumentation, it is possible to specify one of the central points for consideration on which the price-maintenance discussion should concentrate in the future.

---

[17] Cf. on this and thereafter Lambert (2009, pp. 1949f) and Vertical GL, paragraph 224.

[18] Cf. Horst (1992, pp. 164 ff).

[19] Cf. for an overview von Weizsäcker (2005, pp. 50ff).

4.5.2 Vertical Price Maintenance Allegedly Leads to Excessively High and Inflexible Prices for All Products

To show that an excessive price level can be achieved by fixed consumer prices, Dobson and Waterson first model a bilateral duopoly at the retailing and manufacturing level. This is referred to in the literature also as *double common agency* (cf. above hub-and-spoke cartels) or *interlocking relationships*.[20] In the model, two manufacturers from two different value chains each deliver to two distributors. The distributors in turn order their goods from the two manufacturers. Because retail prices are predefined, improved purchasing terms and conditions cannot be passed on to consumers. For this reason, a distributor cannot strengthen his own competitive position in competition using price-setting measures, so that there is less incentive for distributors to negotiate with manufacturers on their ex-works prices. The consequence is a reduction in the intensity of competition at the manufacturer level and, therefore, higher retail prices. If the industry, when setting prices, additionally uses fixed components (e.g. franchise fees), then, according to Rey and Vergé, industry-wide monopoly prices may even result.[21] Biscourp et al. base this theory on their empirical results after the introduction of the Loi Galland in France in 1996, a statute which effectively legitimised industry-wide minimum-price maintenance. There were increases particularly in those prices which had previously been relatively low; the correlation between the intensity of local competition and the locally observed selling prices declined.[22] In contrast, it was found, after the abolition of price maintenance for books in the United Kingdom that prices fell and the choice of titles even increased.[23]

Moreover, resale price maintenance could also contribute towards safeguarding the monopoly profits of a few manufacturers operating in a market de facto as monopolists. This could be explained, first of all, by easier price discrimination against different buyer groups because, using a high maintained resale price, it would be possible to influence the sale of goods acquired for relatively favourable prices to customer groups willing to pay a higher price.[24] Moreover, resale price maintenance could act as self-binding instrument with which the manufacturer could bind himself to the price that offers him maximum profit. In this way, he could credibly persuade the purchasing distributor that he would not conclude any

---

[20] Cf. Dobson and Waterson (2007) and Rey and Vergé (2008).

[21] Cf. Rey and Vergé (2008).

[22] Cf. Biscourp et al. (2008), additionally also a report by a committee of experts led by Guy Carnivet 'Restaurer la concurrence par les prix—Les produits de grande consommation et les relations entre industrie et commerce', 2004, p. 60. http://www.ladocumentationfrancaise.fr/rapports-publics/044000494/index.shtml and http://www.finances.gouv.fr/directions_services/cedef/synthese/loi_galland/synthese.htm.

[23] Cf. Office of Fair Trading (2008).

[24] Cf. Bowman (1955, pp. 839f) and Overstreet (1983, pp. 33ff).

other contracts at more favourable terms with other distributors. The effect would be that any higher purchase quantity of a distributor in the market could be sold to consumers only at a lower price.[25]

The German Government provided further indications of excessive pricing through vertical price maintenance in the run-up to the prohibition of price maintenance in 1973. After shutting out (price) competition between distributors, manufacturers would frequently compete for distributors by means of discounts. This competition would either drive the margins even higher or inhibit intended margin reductions by cementing the consumer price that should actually have been adjusted.[26] According to the Federal Government, fixed manufacturer prices would have to be calculated in such a way that market fluctuations and those in the cost structure, could be compensated for, even by the weakest distribution enterprises still considered necessary for sales. Prices would normally be calculated in such a way that particularly cost increases could be compensated for over a longer period of time. For the reasons given above, maintained prices in many cases remained unchanged at too high a level for many years.

Criticism of vertical price maintenance is further supported by the fact that the effects on the price level described in this section would affect not only price-maintained articles, but could also influence the entire price structure in a market. 'Where distributors are able to compete on price for non-price-maintained goods, such competition will be in fact lessened depending on the dissemination of price-maintained branded articles within a sector, because the maintained prices of the branded goods often serve as a guide for the price calculation of non-branded goods. [...] Some retailers welcome maintained prices, especially for low-price articles, as a desirable aid to price calculation.'[27] According to this argument, the market clearance process could be regarded as distorted, because sufficient price variations do not occur. Excess returns are not based on surpluses of demand or capacity bottlenecks, but would be the result of monopoly-type supplier structures. For this reason, the normalisation of returns could also no longer function in the same way as in free markets.

It can also be stated with regard to the assumed effects of excessive and inflexible prices through price maintenance, that these are only conceivable in extreme situations involving

- inflexible fixed-price maintenance systems,
- a very high market share of price-maintained articles and
- monopoly-type supply structures.

---

25 Cf. O'Brien and Shaffer (1992), Rey and Vergé (2004), Hart and Tirole (1990) and Vertical GL, paragraph 224.

26 Cf. German Bundestag (1962, p. 26).

27 German Bundestag (1962, p. 29) (translated from German).

If, on the other hand, there is sufficiently effective inter-brand competition, i.e. no insurmountable barriers to market entry or monopolising effects, all of these lines of argument disappear.

4.6 Conclusion on the Risk Potential of Admissible Price Restraints

To summarise the above-mentioned arguments, supporters of strict blanket RPM prohibition quote the hypotheses listed in Fig. 4.1 in order to underline their position.

However, it was found for each of the assumed effects given that they can be plausibly explained only in exceptional cases. No general and enduring reduction in welfare and distortion of competition as a consequence of vertical price coordination in the value chain could be proven until now. In many market situations, the exact opposite is the case. If at all, the negative effects appear to be explained only in the cases described at the outset as a 'nightmare scenario' characterised as follows:

- Essential goods that are urgently needed.
- Markets that are completely stagnant and barely innovative.
- Almost insurmountable barriers to market entry.
- High market coverage by inflexible fixed-price maintenance systems.

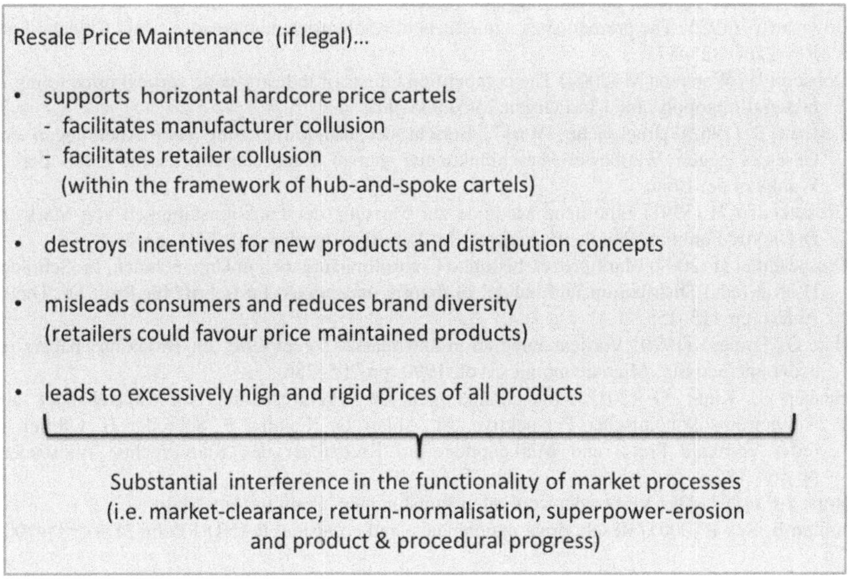

Fig. 4.1 Hypotheses on dangers of inflexible fixed-price maintenance

A qualitative survey in the consumer-goods sector[28] shows that inflexible fixed-price maintenance systems are not currently desired by branded-article manufacturers or by major trading systems. It is more a matter of the more circumspect and less far-reaching forms of vertical price coordination and brand care in internal competition of the value systems. The assumed competition-distorting effects of legal RPM do not apply to them. This is because they serve the sole purpose of preventing the worst excesses of price wars and brand vandalism and promoting value-adding efficiency by means of vertical cooperation (e.g. as part of category management), the latter not least also to the benefit of consumers.

References

Angland J (2008) Resale price maintenance in the United States: a review and prognosis. In: Competition law international, Feb 2008, pp 27–35

Bennett M, Fletcher A, Giovannetti E, Stallibrass D (2010) Resale price maintenance: explaining the controversy, and small steps towards a more nuanced policy, MPRA paper. http://mpra.ub.unimuenchen.de/21121/1/MPRA_paper_21121.pdf. Accessed 11 Feb 2011

Bernheim BD, Whinston MD (1985) Common marketing agency as a device for facilitating collusion. RAND J Econ 16(2):269–281

Biscourp P, Boutin X, Vergé T (2008) The effects of retail regulations on prices: evidence from the loi galland. http://www.diw.de/sixcms/detail.php/86155. Accessed 06 Dec 2011

Blechman M (2012) Unreasonable Restraints of Trade. Die Entwicklung der Rechtsprechung zum Preisbindungsverbot in den USA. In: Ahlert D, Kenning P, Schröder H, Olbrich R (eds) Vertikale Preis- und Markenpflege im Kreuzfeuer des Kartellrechts, Wiesbaden, pp 199–204

Borchert M, Grossekettler H (1985) Preis- und Wettbewerbstheorie: Marktprozesse als analytisches Problem und ordnungspolitische Gestaltungsaufgabe. Stuttgart inter alia

Bowman W (1955) The prerequisites and effects of resale price maintenance. Univ Chicago Law Rev 22(4):825–873

Dobson PW, Waterson M (2007) The competition effects of industry-wide vertical price fixing in bilateral oligopoly. Int J Ind Organ 25(5):935–962

German B (1962) Drucksache IV/617, Bericht der Bundesregierung über Änderungen des Gesetzes gegen Wettbewerbsbeschränkungen gemäß Bundestagsdrucksache 2886 der 3, Wahlperiode, Bonn

Grossekettler H (1991) Eine neue Methode zur Messung der Funktionsfähigkeit von Märkten: Die KMK-Funktionsfähigkeits-Analyse. In: Die Betriebswirtschaft 4/91, pp 46 ff

Grossekettler H (2009) Marktprozessbedingte Controllingaufgaben in Unternehmen. In: Schröder H et al (eds) Distribution und handel in theorie und praxis. Festschrift für Prof. Dr. Dieter Ahlert, pp 115–155

Hart O, Tirole J (1990) Vertical integration and market foreclosure. In: Brookings papers on economic activity. Microeconomics, vol. 1990. pp 205–286

Haucap J, Klein G (2012) Einschränkungen der Preisgestaltung im Einzelhandel aus wettbewerbsökonomischer Perspektive. In: Ahlert D, Kenning P, Schröder H, Olbrich R (eds) Vertikale Preis- und Markenpflege im Kreuzfeuer des Kartellrechts, Wiesbaden, pp 169–186

Horst J-P (1992) Das Verbot der vertikalen Preisbindung, Frankfurt am Main

Jullien B, Rey P (2007) Resale price maintenance and collusion. RAND J Econ 38(4):983–1001

[28] Cf. Schefer (2013) (forthcoming).

Lambert T (2009) Dr. Miles is dead. Now what?: structuring a rule of reason for evaluating minimum resale price maintenance. William and Mary Law Rev 50(6): 1937–1977
Lorenz C (2006) Marktscreening nach Kartellstrukturen. Ein Verfahren zur Kartellaufdeckung auf Basis des Koordinationsmängel-Diagnosekonzepts (KMD-Kartellcheck); Hamburg
Mathewson F, Winter R (1998) The Law and Economics of Resale Price Maintenance. In: Review of Industrial Organization, vol 13, no. 1–2, pp 57–84
McLaughlin A (1979) An economic analysis of resale price maintenance. Dissertation, University of California, Los Angeles
Möschel W (2012) Zwecke der Preisempfehlung. Die Motive des Gesetzgebers. In: Ahlert D, Kenning P, Schröder H, Olbrich R (eds) Vertikale Preis- und Markenpflege im Kreuzfeuer des Kartellrechts, Wiesbaden, pp 193–198
O'Brien DP, Shaffer G (1992) Vertical control with bilateral contracts. RAND J Econ 23(3): 299–308
Office Of Fair Trading (2008): An evaluation of the impact upon productivity of ending resale price maintenance on books. Report prepared for the OFT by the Centre for Competition Policy at University of East Anglia, http://www.oft.gov.uk/shared_oft/economic_research/oft981.pdf. Accessed 06 Dec 2011
Overstreet T (1983) Resale price maintenance: economic theories and empirical evidence. Bureau of economics staff report to the federal trade commission
Rey P, Vergé T (2004) Bilateral control with vertical contracts. RAND J Econ 35(4):728–746
Rey P, Vergé T (2008) Resale price maintenance and interlocking relationships. J Ind Econ 58(4):928–961
Schefer B (2013) Das Verbot der vertikalen Preisbindung, forthcoming
Schwalbe U (2012) Wettbewerbsökonomische Aspekte der Preisbindung in Wertschöpfungsketten. In: Ahlert D, Kenning P, Schröder H, Olbrich R (eds) Vertikale Preis- und Markenpflege im Kreuzfeuer des Kartellrechts, Wiesbaden, pp 155–168
Shaffer G (1991) Slotting allowances and resale price maintenance: a comparison of facilitating practices. RAND J Econ 22(1):120–135
Simon S (2012) Preisbindungen und Preisempfehlungen. Kartellrechtliche Grenzen der vertikalen Kooperation zwischen Industrie und Handel. In: Ahlert D, Kenning P, Schröder H, Olbrich R (eds) Vertikale Preis- und Markenpflege im Kreuzfeuer des Kartellrechts, Wiesbaden, pp 249–256
Telser LG (1960) Why should manufacturers want fair trade? J Law Econ 3:86–105
Von Weizsäcker C (2005) Marktzutrittsschranken. In: Oberender P (ed) Effizienz und Wettbewerb, Berlin, pp 43–61
Wey C (2012) Preisempfehlungen aus wettbewerbsökonomischer Sicht. In: Ahlert D, Kenning P, Schröder H, Olbrich R (eds) Vertikale Preis- und Markenpflege im Kreuzfeuer des Kartellrechts, Wiesbaden, pp 221–226

Chapter 5
Competition-Policy Implications

The above statements reveal conflicting arguments on the subject of RPM prohibition:

On the one hand, the deregulation of this statutory prohibition is recommended without delay. This is combined with the hope that the abolition of legal restrictions on price formation will increase the diversity of supply. This would result in price-maintained offers competing locally for the favour of consumers alongside non-price-maintained offers, and if appropriate, also with recommended retail prices.

On the other hand, there is a risk that allowing price-formation processes would lead to the markets being 'totally contaminated' by inflexible fixed-price maintenance systems. This could promote the formation of hardcore price cartels in horizontal competition.

This raises the issue of compromise, i.e. whether there could be an *optimum relationship between price-maintained, price-cared and non-price maintained products* in accordance with the competition-policy principle. If so, this raises the next question as to whether this can, and should be, prescribed by law.

5.1 On the Question of the Optimum Combination of Price-Formation Processes in the Light of the Competition-Policy Principle

Figure 5.1 presents a possible connection between the market share of price-maintained products and welfare deriving from the extent of supply diversity.

The first part of the figure is characterised by the fact that no price restraints exist, e.g. because they have not been admissible until now. However, the fact cannot be overlooked that the RPM prohibition applies only partially, namely only to free and cooperating value systems. In contrast, distribution systems organised on a hierarchical basis have always been able to prescribe centrally controlled prices and, as a result, implement their pricing concepts without legal restrictions.

D. Ahlert and B. Schefer, *Vertical Price Coordination and Brand Care*, SpringerBriefs in Business, DOI: 10.1007/978-3-642-35570-7_5,

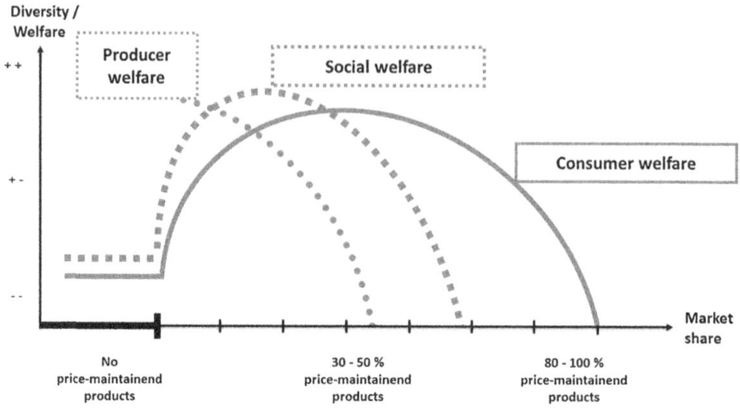

Fig. 5.1 Optimal level of resale price maintenance

To this extent, the phenomenon of maintained prices can arise already in the first segment of the curve.

If RPM prohibition were to be abolished and the consumer generally allowed to choose between price-maintained, price-cared and non-price-maintained products, this would initially result in a greater diversity of supply than if he were to continue to be denied the freedom to choose. Enlarging the admissible alternative scope means (at least potentially) an enhancement of 'consumer welfare'. As the number of price-maintained offers grows, the diversity can also increase, because price-maintained products are likely to encourage non-price-maintained competition. The market volume in this goods category would increase, also improving the range of alternatives for consumers.

With a certain degree (but not known precisely) of market coverage by price-maintained products, the zenith of these effects is achieved. The Guidelines on Vertical Restraints of the European Commission (paragraph 79) define the safe level for parallel networks of similar vertical restraints as 50 % of the relevant market. It may well be the case that, with this percentage, maximum consumer welfare has been achieved, also in the case of price-maintenance systems. The resulting key issues are evident:

- What happens when this limit is exceeded?
- Does it cause market failure?
- Does coverage of the market with price-maintenance systems result in supply rigidity at manufacturing and retailing levels and innovation fatigue?
- Are high barriers to market entry the consequence?

Nobody knows the answers to these questions, because apart from some non-representative exceptions, systems of fixed-price maintenance have not been admissible in Germany since 1973 and, for this reason, cannot be observed with regard to their effects on competition and welfare. In the event that competition is (sufficiently) effective, *complete market stagnation as a consequence of abolishing*

RPM prohibition must be regarded as highly unlikely. It is hardly conceivable that suppliers in a market with a high share of price-maintained products (e.g. more than one third) would feel the need to establish other price-maintenance systems, primarily because *consumers would probably or even definitely not accept* them. The marginal utility of each additional introduction of a maintenance system would fall, as illustrated by the function of 'Producer Welfare' in Fig. 5.1. As an equilibrium, a stable solution could settle at the point where the sum of consumer welfare and producer welfare reaches its maximum, i.e. 'social welfare'.

Whether declining marginal utility can be more than compensated for by the advantages of collusive behaviour allegedly made possible by price-maintenance systems within a group of oligopolies—whether this takes place at industrial level or distributor level or even at both levels—has not been proven by any survey to date. It appears plausible only in the case of a pre-existing market failure (with insurmountable market entry barriers). However, in this case, it would be a matter for competition policy to eliminate the *causes* of market failure.

5.2 Need for Amendment of Block Exemption Regulations: The Case-by-Case Approach

The conclusion to be drawn from the above statements is that *optimum welfare relations between the alternative price-formation systems definitely prevail,* but they are likely to differ in the various goods categories. However, they are not capable of diagnosis or forecast and, for this reason, *should under no circumstances be prescribed by the State.* Giving the participants in the sales channels back their freedom of action would enable effective competition (as a process of discovery) to pursue these optima.

The minimum that should take place for the purpose of deregulation is the *detachment of price maintenance from hardcore restraints* ('Kernbeschränkungen') in the block exemption regulations.[1] This is because it is already questionable whether price restraints, by definition, constitute restraints of competition.[2]

---

[1] Cf. Article 4 of the Block Exemption Regulation 2010 (Restrictions that remove the benefit of the block exemption—hardcore restrictions).

The exemption provided for in Article 2 shall not apply to vertical agreements which, directly or indirectly, in isolation or in combination with other factors under the control of the parties, have as their object:(a) the restriction of the buyer's ability to determine its sale price, without prejudice to the possibility of the supplier to impose a maximum sale price or recommend a sale price, provided that they do not amount to a fixed or minimum sale price as a result of pressure from, or incentives offered by, any of the parties [...]. Cf. also paragraph 47ff of the European Guidelines on Vertical Restraints (2010).

[2] The term 'vertical restraint' is at least misleading (and has possibly contributed towards making vertical price maintenance a taboo subject). Thus also Möschel (2010, p. 1229): 'Restraints of competition can only exist within competitive relations. They do not exist in vertical cooperations, in agreements within supplier–buyer chains. It would be more precise to

If, contrary to expectations, the market share of price-maintained goods should exceed a percentage to be defined (e.g. 50 %), then it is necessary to research the *causes and effects* of this phenomenon. If this created a risk of fostering horizontal price cartels, it would still be possible to express *a partial RPM prohibition* as the ultima ratio.[3]

It is necessary to reiterate that price-maintenance systems were inadmissible already prior to 1973, *if introduced by dominant companies*. This rule could be re-introduced. Article 3 of the Block Exemption Regulation 2010 must also be taken into account, which makes exemption dependent on the market share threshold of the supplier/buyer not exceeding 30 %.

Given the largely pro-competitive effects of vertical price coordination in the normal case, there appears to be an urgent need at the present time to *abolish the per-se prohibition* of price restraints. A differentiating rule which limits a prohibition statute to certain critical situations is referred to as a *case-by-case* approach. It may also be considered a deregulation compromise. What 'critical situations' could be meant in this case? The decisive factor is the existence of a substantial risk to the effectiveness of *inter*-brand competition. To make this clear, we again consider the abovementioned (fictitious) extreme scenario:

> Imagine a market in which urgently needed essential goods are traded. For this reason, consumers cannot avoid this market by abstention. The market is dominated by a tight oligopoly of suppliers, is completely stagnant, barely innovative and there are insurmountable barriers to entry.

Under the principle of effective market processes, such circumstances could justifiably be referred to as a 'nightmare scenario of complete market failure'. This represents the first case where the need to retain the prohibition of price maintenance appears clear and compelling. However, even in such an extreme situation, it is questionable whether the price restraint can be revealed to be the *cause of market failure or* whether the imposition of price-maintenance prohibition can be regarded as merely treating *the symptoms*.

When defining the 'critical situations', however, consideration must be given not only to a situation of complete market failure. Additionally, a prohibition, or at

---

(Footnote 2 continued)
talk of vertical ties, rather than vertical restraints on competition. In many legal systems, the terminology is confusing. However, this is not due to a competition theory view, but to the randomness of history. 'Purely vertical restraints' cannot restrict competition. At best, they promote the same with regard to competing products (inter-brand competition). This statement no longer applies without qualification, if the vertical tie has spillover effects, if it results in horizontal effects. One example is a vertical price tie used as an instrument to facilitate an agreement at manufacturer level or at retailer level. A horizontal effect is also the potential raising of barriers to market entry, e.g. based on sole distribution and sole purchase contracts. In the event of vertical ties with simultaneously existing horizontal effects, the pro-competitive effects associated with the vertical ties do not simply disappear. From a competition policy point of view, it may be necessary to weigh the pro-competitive effects against the anti-competitive effects' (translated from German).

[3] As already explained in detail by Horst in (1992).

least a special examination for the purpose of abuse control (rule-of-reason approach), could also be considered, if individual risk factors existed (in the sense of assumptions capable of being disproved), for example, in the case of:

- market-dominating companies as initiators of inflexible fixed resale price maintenance systems,
- markets with a very high market share of price-tied products, e.g. more than 50 %,[4]
- a market structure with a high probability of collusive behaviour 'which is characterised by comparably few companies, between which there is a certain degree of symmetry, above all with regard to market shares, the market is transparent and a credible sanction mechanism is available',[5]
- Situations in which the desire for price maintenance emanates from distributors,[6]
- Essential goods that are urgently needed and which consumers cannot avoid purchasing.

It is obvious that these cases require more in-depth economic discussion.

To prepare for an amendment of the Block Exemption Regulation, the *interpretation of the rules by the Guidelines on Vertical Restraints* must initially be regarded as in need of examination. Regular revision appears necessary, because the guidelines are expressly described as not 'carved in stone'; instead it says in paragraph 4: 'The Commission will continue to monitor the operation of the Block Exemption Regulation and Guidelines based on market information from stakeholders and national competition authorities and may revise this notice in the light of future developments and evolving insights.'

---

[4] An equivalent is found in Art. 6 of Vertical Block Exemption Regulation. According thereto: 'the Commission may by regulation declare that, where parallel networks of similar vertical restraints cover more than 50% of a relevant market, this Regulation shall not apply [...]', (cf. also paragraph 79 of the European Guidelines on Vertical Restraints 2010).

[5] Schwalbe (2012, p. 166) (translated from German).

[6] According to Schwalbe (2012, p. 166 ff) 'the party that wishes the price restraint could be of importance for the assessment of the effects of a price restraint...If, for example, a manufacturer of a product competing with many other manufacturers of close substitutes, wishes to prescribe the retail price by price maintenance, then it is to be expected that the price restraint will tend to raise efficiency. Moreover, if the relevant product is also not a 'strong' brand and consumers are generally prepared to acquire comparable products from other manufacturers, then it can be assumed that price maintenance can be regarded as more positive for competition. Under German competition law and its adaption to European competition law, price restraints could be exempted in such cases. However, if there are only a few distributors who stock a certain product and if they ask the manufacturers to set the ultimate-consumer price, and if the product is a strong brand, i.e. intra-brand competition is crucial, then a price restraint would be expected to have the effect of limiting competition between the distributors. The result of this is that a small quantity is offered at high prices and, consequently, the position of consumers is worsened. In such a case, a price restraint should be prohibited as harmful to competition' (translated from German).

Regulations, guidelines and official practice of the cartel authorities must be examined in terms of deregulation, when new knowledge emerges. Conveying this fact is the intention of the present publication.

5.3 Per-se Prohibition Versus Rule of Reason: From the Defence of Efficiency to the Defence of Effectiveness

One of the repeated objections to the deregulation postulation as expressed above is that the legislator had, through *defending efficiency*, allowed business practice enough freedom to enforce legitimate interests against economically ineffective intervention on the part of the competition authorities. A rule-of- reason standard had existed in Europe long before the Leegin judgment in the USA in 2007. The *individual exemption* created in sec. 2 (1) Act against Restraints of Competition (GWB) or in Art. 101 (3) TFEU provides that the competition authorities and courts can, in proceedings against companies and groups of companies, allow a convincingly reasoned efficiency defence as justification and thereupon waive further prosecution of the incriminating behaviour (e.g. of a vertical price agreement).

The defence of efficiency is however, *a defect from an economic perspective* for the following reasons:

- According to sec. 2 (1) GWB, the entrepreneur must prove that an additional profit is clearly attributable to the incriminating behaviour and that the consumer was (is, will be) reasonably involved therein. It is common knowledge among commercial accounting experts that no such proof can normally be provided.
- Moreover, from an economic point of view, it is not primarily a matter of the monetary profit for the period, but of sustainable consumer welfare over an extended period of time. The greatest conceivable benefit to consumers is the effectiveness of competition processes and not market structures or market results that simply appear advantageous.
- The entrepreneur must prove that the incriminating behaviour contributes towards improving the production or distribution of goods or promotes technical or economic progress and that no restraints are imposed on the participating companies that are not indispensable for achieving these aims. To provide clear evidence of a beneficial contribution, it would be necessary, inter alia, to know the optimum market results. Nevertheless, in view of the complexity of dynamic economic and competition processes, this exceeds the human capacity for perception and judgment and is regarded in economics as the 'pretence of knowledge'.
- The entrepreneur must prove that the incriminating behaviour cannot exclude the competition with respect to the goods affected. From an economic perspective, this requirement (similar to those in the above points) is almost unsurpassed in terms of naivety. Because, based on the statements made in this

article, the circumstances under which the critical practices in question here are capable of obstructing, restraining or falsifying competition (as defined in sec. 1 GWB) has not even been clarified theoretically and, presumably, cannot be clarified. How should a practical businessperson thus provide evidence on such issues?

- Only for the sake of completeness is attention drawn to the fact that the price of 'absolution in the individual case' is unreasonably high. To be considered, inter alia, are the hordes of competition lawyers whom the business person would have to consult in order to bring the defence of efficiency before the competition authorities and then, in case of doubt, also before the courts, quite apart from the matter of the costs of business experts (controlling, consumer research).
- The greatest harm caused by this defence of efficiency lies for the business person in the risk of incurring costs (lack of certainty with regard to fines, loss of reputation and civil-law claims for damages by allegedly affected parties), also because of the time sequence of events.

  - First of all, the actions potentially of relevance for cartel law must be performed—for example, vertical coordination of price structuring.
  - Then incrimination could be (but need not be) undertaken by one of the numerous potentially responsible competition authorities.
  - Only then can the entrepreneur seek 'absolution' based on the defence of efficiency.
  - Until a final decision by the authorities and courts is obtained after many years, a commercially unacceptable degree of uncertainty for planning and legal purposes will prevail.

For the reasons outlined above, the defence of efficiency can be regarded only to a very limited extent as a suitable and economically acceptable remedy against the cartel-law (over) regulation of consumer-goods distribution.

There can be no talk of any de facto rule-of-reason standard. Instead, the per-se prohibition of price maintenance prevails in Europe as before. In our view, there is an acute need for deregulation, *de lege ferenda.*

Since amending of the pertinent legal statutes takes time or will possibly not happen at all, this raises the question of what can be done (in the interim) under applicable law, i.e. *de lege lata*.

Interpreting of the construct of individual exemption obviously places *too much emphasis on* 'efficiency'. Short-term (operating) cost-and-benefit effects of entrepreneurial (or also State) measures are undoubtedly important, but are not the decisive categories of economic thought. Of primary importance are the *long-term (strategic) criteria of* 'effectiveness'. This should be noted when, in the more recent debate on competition theory, consideration is repeatedly given to the optimisation of *efficiency-oriented competition policy* in the trade-off between two

Effectiveness \ Efficiency	**Type I Error** Punish legal behavior	**Type II Error** Not punish illegal behavior
Type A Error Restrain economically beneficial behavior		Maximise Type II Error
Type B Error Permit economically harmful behavior	Maximise Type I Error	

Fig. 5.2 Effectiveness of legal norms and efficiency of implementation

possible fault types. A Type I error means prohibiting admissible acts whereas a Type II error consists of failing to prosecute inadmissible acts. Both errors are attributable to incomplete information.[7]

By reference to the intervention by the State and its authorities, it is a question of additionally reflecting on an *effectiveness-oriented optimisation of economic policy*. It is necessary to distinguish between two further types of errors: A Type A error means a legal provision prohibits economically advantageous behaviour, whereas a Type B error consists of permitting economically damaging behaviour. The RPM prohibition obviously concerns an economic policy error of Type A.

If the effectiveness- and efficiency-oriented observations were put next to each other in a matrix (cf. Fig. 5.2), strange conclusions could be drawn. It makes no difference how efficiently breaches against a certain legal provision are prosecuted (e.g. by a competition authority), if the legal provision itself is ineffective (Type A error). It would be more advantageous to welfare if the authority were to commit a Type II error, namely not to prosecute the inadmissible acts under the (erroneous) legal provision. However, before the authorities come to believe that they have been persuaded to undertake potentially unlawful behaviour as a result of these statements, it is necessary to draw attention to the following facts: only rarely are the pertinent legal provisions structured in such a way that they clearly prohibit behaviour of economic subjects that is conducive to optimising consumer welfare. Thus says Möschel[8]: 'It would be wrong to argue here that the Federal Cartel Office was bound by the law and had absolutely no scope of action. The indefinite

[7] 'If the maximization of welfare is declared as an aim of competition policy, competition policy decisions must be explicitly based on forecasts of effects, ultimately on cost-benefit analyses (performance test). What happens if one is wrong? This is a legitimate question, but one that must also be asked of orthodox competition policy. It is also reliant on forecasts. Both can be wrong; both may commit Type 1 or Type 2 errors, i.e. prohibit an admissible act (Type 1 error) and fail to prosecute an inadmissible act (Type 2 error). The decisive question is: what form of competition policy has a higher error probability and what are the costs of erroneous decisions—measured in terms of lost welfare?' Schmidtchen (2005, p. 30) (translated from German).

[8] Möschel (2010, p. 1231) (translated from German).

legal concepts of competition law which are intended to allow adjustment of the case law to business life as it develops, allow cartel authorities and courts a sufficient degree of flexibility.'

In conclusion, there is nothing to prevent the competition authorities from *putting an effectiveness defence before an efficiency defence,* in which economically advantageous behaviour—and this clearly includes vertical price and brand management in value systems—is not rendered incriminating in certain situations or cases, and this fact is communicated with binding effect to the relevant market operators.

5.4 Conclusions on Competition-Policy and Cartel-Law

If the competition processes of a market are confirmed as effective, there is absolutely *no* justification for cartel-law intervention in value-adding processes. In this case, the prohibition of vertical price maintenance per-se is misguided. If, instead, market efficacy is distorted, the *causes* of market failure must be analysed and remedied using competition policy. In case of doubt, these are ultimately excessively high barriers to market entry. No insurmountable barriers to market entry can be created by vertical coordination in the form of price and brand care. On the contrary, they can help to tear down such barriers.

It becomes dangerous for the effectiveness of competition in tight oligopoly markets, if inflexible fixed-price maintenance systems gain a very large market share. Only then can the abolition of the RPM prohibition under certain circumstances have negative effects on horizontal inter-brand competition—in particular by promoting price cartels. Although consumers, with increasing market coverage by price-maintained goods, would increasingly wish to switch to non-price-maintained products, they could not do so if there were almost insurmountable barriers to market entry. If consumers were also unable to not buy at all (e.g. for essential goods), then, and *only then*, does the situation arise in which a partial RPM prohibition could be considered on competition policy grounds as the ultima ratio.

If one asks in general terms whether restoring the freedom of action in competition generally raises or lowers diversity (desirable in competition policy), and whether, for this reason, degrees of freedom should be narrowed or widened, one is confronted with *two diametrically opposing points of view.*

- There is great acceptance of the theory that *non-State-regulated practices of participants in consumer-goods distribution substantially reduce supply diversity.* This is because the conduct of competitors released from State control could result in the formation of monopolies. This normally reduces consumer welfare. Moreover, the case could arise in which small and medium-size companies (SMEs) no longer had any chance of survival, no matter how attractive their supply concepts. Consequently, they need protection against the abuse of power, i.e. it is necessary to narrow the degree of freedom.

- But the counter-theory also appears plausible: *The better way* to prevent uncontrolled competitive behaviour, i.e. to avoid the formation of monopolies in the sector *is self-help measures of the economy*. State attempts to regulate the vertical relations between manufacturing and retailing had always failed until now. Grounds: Ultimately it is a matter of the litmus test for the consumer. The diversity offered is not an end in itself, but could only survive to the extent it is accepted (i.e. demanded) by consumers. For this reason, participants in the value systems—including also the SMEs—have to be given the freedom to ensure that their supply concepts could be presented at the consumer level (i.e. across all levels of distribution) in unadulterated form. This results in the demand for the expansion of the scope of action in vertical marketing.

The two lines of argument presented above may be understandable and possibly also correct, but they refer to *different subject areas*.

- The theory on the risks of monopolisation and the suppression of efficient supply concepts (theory of impoverishment) refers to *horizontal inter-brand competition*. In this area, *State regulation has undoubtedly proved to be necessary and useful*—and could even be made more strict or improved. This is largely concerned with avoiding restraints and distortions of competition by horizontal price cartels. However, consideration must also be given to distortions of change, selection and imitation processes within the framework of innovation and diffusion of new and established supply concepts. This means abusive behaviour in the sense of dynamic market domination.[9]
- The counter-theory of the innovation-promoting effect of expanding of the freedom of action and control (enrichment theory) refers to the processes within value systems, i.e. to the *intra-brand relationships between manufacturing and retailing*. Bringing attractive supply concepts to the consumer level effectively and efficiently via vertical marketing requires a strict, consistent control of processes in the value systems by the participants themselves, but not by the State. *This freedom of action and control should not only be legally admissible, but should also be protected by the State*—e.g. by proprietary rights, protected freedom of contract, protection against abusive behaviour of third parties etc.

As long as it remains unclear which of the controversial positions will prevail, there is a *considerable legal uncertainty*. The diversity of current announcements, guidelines and regulations and their interpretation by the European competition authorities have not yet achieved the degree of maturity necessary to retain or even

[9] Market power of relevance for competition policy can be defined as the ability to systematically distort market processes. This concerns the potential—and not just the process involving the so-called abusive exploitation of this potential—of an economic subject or several economic subjects (e.g. of an oligopoly acting collusively), to influence the market processes—possibly in the course of a dynamic, cumulative process—in such a way that ultimately the conditions for effectiveness of the market system are completely disabled. Cf. Ahlert and Wellmann (1988a, b) for more details.

render stricter the hitherto practised official implementation of cartel-law regulations in the area of vertical marketing.

There is a risk that the forms of intervention currently under consideration would *not promote* the efficient operation of the markets, *but stifle* them.

References

Ahlert D, Wellmann T (1988a) Deregulierung oder Verschärfung des GWB?—Wettbewerbspolitische und wettbewerbsrechtliche Konsequenzen der Konzentration im Handel. In: BFuP (Betriebswirtschaftliche Forschung und Praxis), No. 03/1988, pp 250–275

Ahlert D, Wellmann T (1988b) Von der Machtkonzentration zur dynamischen Marktbeherrschung im Handel—Wirtschaftswissenschaftliche Grundlagen einer Diskussion zur Kartellrechtsnovelle. In: BFuP (Betriebswirtschaftliche Forschung und Praxis), No. 03/1988, pp 193–219

European Commission (2010) Guidelines on vertical restraints (Text with EEA relevance) (2010 / C 130 / 01)

Horst J-P (1992) Das Verbot der vertikalen Preisbindung. Frankfurt am Main

Möschel W (2010) Markenartikel und vertikale Kooperation. In: Wirtschaft und Wettbewerb, No 12, pp 1229–1237

Schmidtchen D (2005) Effizienz als Leitbild der Wettbewerbspolitik: Für einen more economic approach. In: Oberender P (ed) Effizienz und Wettbewerb, Berlin, pp 9–41

Schwalbe U (2012) Wettbewerbsökonomische Aspekte der Preisbindung in Wertschöpfungsketten. In: Ahlert D, Kenning P, Schröder H, Olbrich R (eds) Vertikale Preis- und Markenpflege im Kreuzfeuer des Kartellrechts, Wiesbaden, pp 155–168

Chapter 6
Management Summary: 'The Liberation of the Value Chain from Cartel-Law Restraints'

6.1 The Controversy Surrounding the Limitation of Freedom of Action in Vertical Marketing

The task of competition policy is to eliminate or to prevent restraints of competition and not to cause them. For this reason, all legal restrictions of entrepreneurial freedom of action in competition must be examined regularly on the *"test bench" of deregulation*. The most recent cartel-law interventions in the vertical coordination of the value chains and the resulting rigid limitation of freedom of action in consumer-goods distribution are currently the subject of controversy and viewed increasingly critically in all related disciplines.

Largely undisputed among economists is that exposing and preventing *horizontal 'hardcore' price cartels* are among the most important tasks of the competition authorities. This is because horizontal price agreements between suppliers (or between demanders) at one and same economic level of a sector can considerably impair the effectiveness of *inter*-brand competition between competing brands. However, there are extreme differences of opinion on *vertical price coordination* in the so-called *intra*-brand sector of a value chain, i.e., between manufacturing and retail companies or between wholesale and retail companies, in each case by reference to one and the same brand. These relate to cases involving not only extensive, inflexible resale price-maintenance systems, but also to less incisive forms of multi-level harmonisation of price and brand management within the value chain. These include frank discussions about useful brand-policy price architectures in sales channels, but also price-maintenance measures which are not the subject of multilateral, but of bilateral or individual agreements. These also include agreements of limited duration on price ranges and special-offer prices.

The *core of this controversy* is the question of whether vertical price coordination within the sales channels exerts serious negative effects on competition and welfare and if it does so, whether this is *fundamental and the normal case*. If this is the case,

Cf. on this whole chapter Ahlert (2012).

D. Ahlert and B. Schefer, *Vertical Price Coordination and Brand Care*, SpringerBriefs in Business, DOI: 10.1007/978-3-642-35570-7_6,

strict prohibition, combined with the threat of high fines, appears inevitable—similar to the case of horizontal price cartels. However, if this is not the case per se, but at most *exceptionally* (under certain conditions in certain situations), then the cartel law that currently applies is urgently in need of amendment. Rigid acts of intervention into freedom of action could then be limited to these exceptional cases. Demonstrating the plausibility of this case-by-case approach is the subject matter of the present article.

6.2 The Liberation of Interdisciplinary Dialogue from Prejudices and Economic Misunderstandings

The current discussion is frequently overshadowed by *handed-down prejudices, professed normative postulates and axioms, and economic misunderstandings* that obstruct consensus-building.

6.2.1 The Distributor Control of Final Consumer Prices: A Law of Nature?

The belief that price sovereignty lies with the distributor 'by nature' is not economically logical. It is high time for this axiom to be rejected for the following reasons. The present-day reality of distribution is such that hierarchical, cooperating and free value systems with differing combinations of risk spreading and decision-making compete for the favour of consumers. Vertically integrated systems (like IKEA or ZARA) compete with contractual dealers, cooperative retailing groups, franchise systems and free (vertical, non-organised) distribution systems. Manufacturers' brands, trademarks, distributors' brands or even network brands can have a decisive effect on supply concepts.

This *competition between systems* has given rise to different system heads as dominant controlling authorities within value systems. Where it is not distributors, but manufacturers or network centres (e.g., franchisors) who act as system heads, it appears naive and absurd for the State to wish to deprive the latter of their freedom to set prices, one of the most important marketing tools. Prescribing solely *distributor*-controlled price-forming processes for multi-level distribution constitutes interference with effective competition as a process of discovery and thus does not conform to the underlying competition policy model.

6.2.2 Intensive Internal Competition Within Value Systems: A Right of Consumers or Distributors?

Markets can be regarded as effective if there is intensive competition on price and performance *between* different products and brands of a sector. This ideal situation is characterised by a diversity of supply concepts, low barriers to market entry for innovative price-performance combinations and a wide range of alternatives for consumers. However, the postulate of a generous range of selection opportunities for consumers does not extend to competition *within* one and the same brand.

The opinion that a general obligation of competition policy is to bring about *intra*-brand competition by force, is based on *an understanding of politics for which there is no economic explanation.* Consumers have no right based on welfare (or moral grounds) to switch from one supplier of such a branded article to other suppliers of the same article. They also have no right to acquire a desirable article elsewhere at aggressive promotional prices or at permanently low prices. What then creates a *right to intra-brand competition within the market economy*?[1]

Distributors also have no legitimate right through competition policy to interfere with the marketing of products by a branded-article manufacturer contrary to the latter's sales-channel policy intentions or to be able to use the same channels as they wish for their own loss-leaders or tie-in offers.[2]

Conclusion: It is not generally the aim of competition policy to promote intensive *intra*-brand competition through legal intervention. Neither consumers nor competing manufacturers and distributors have any 'God-given' right to limit of freedom of action in consumer-goods distribution.

6.2.3 Large Quantities of Goods at Low Prices: A Reflection of Consumer Welfare and Principle of Competition Policy?

A misunderstanding with probably the most serious consequences in the current controversy is evident in two widely propagated and intermeshed assumptions:

---

[1] Take the example of the Lindt Gold Bunny: it must be noted that chocolate Easter bunnies are on sale at both high and low prices, under famous brand names and as private labels (trademarks) in the most varied range of sizes and flavours, in all food shops and even at petrol stations. Why should the consumer then have a right to switch to alternatives within the 'gold bunny' brand? Even if there were only one single manufacturer that mastered the technique of making hollow chocolate components, it would be absurd to want to regulate this market. The consumer could switch e.g., to a bar of chocolate or box of chocolates instead. In the event of rising prices, the consumer could also simply choose not to consume and thereby 'disempower' the supplier.

[2] If we take high-quality fashion labels like Boss or Bogner as an example, even if fashion outlets stocking these labels focus their sales policy on the quality of their services and not on the prices, they nevertheless rely on the fact that consumers believe that the prices are fair. Consumers take great care to avoid being exploited in terms of price. Low-priced offers of distributors with aggressive pricing policies for clothing labels just purchased by the consumer in his own fashion outlet for the normal price cause an almost irremediable feeling of having been 'ripped off'. Even if the specialist trade were able to match the special price of an aggressive price competitor without delay or immediately remove the product from the list, the 'preconceived notion of an extortionate price' deeply rooted in consumer minds has long since been revived.

1. Reduced prices and increasing quantities within a specific market are a valid indicator of an increase in consumer welfare and, at the same time, of the improved efficiency of competition.

From an economic and consumer-policy perspective, market results in the form of price-quantity ratios for *individual* products are an obviously flawed indicator of consumer welfare. If quantitative market results are to be of any significance, it is necessary to focus on the *long-term development of the price level of all products in a relevant market.* The more heterogeneous the quality of various products over time, the more difficult it is to draw conclusions from individual prices about welfare developments. The *qualitative* characteristics of a market are more important to the consumer than *quantitative* market results (price-quantity ratios). Consumers derive the greatest possible welfare when the effectiveness of competition between alternative price-performance combinations is assured and, for this reason, there is a *diverse range of supply concepts over time*. There should be not only different levels of quality, brands and forms of distribution, but also *different price-formation methods that compete with each other* for the favour of consumers.

Changes in market results are unsuitable as indicators of welfare because, in order to determine welfare gains or losses, the *optimum* market results would have to be known. However, one cannot know the optimum market results, i.e., which qualities, prices and quantities yield optimal welfare. Such a claim would thus constitute a 'pretence of knowledge'. Market results occur as a result of *competition as a process of discovery*. If competitive processes operate perfectly, the resulting price-quantity ratios are, *by definition, optimum in terms of competition and welfare*, regardless of the manner in which they develop.

2. Allowing vertical resale price maintenance would normally result in price increases for popular branded goods.

The myth of the price-driving effects of vertical price maintenance is remarkably enduring. Here too, the focus should not only be on the price level of *price-maintained* products, but on the ongoing development of the price level of *all products in a relevant market.* Allowing price maintenance—in the event of (sufficiently) effective inter-brand competition—does not, under any circumstances, lead to a flood of price restraints and, in the normal case, there is no danger of price increases that will reduce welfare. [3]

[3] See also the chairman of the monopoly commission (Germany): 'To be considered is the fact that vertical price maintenance, in contrast to horizontal agreements, does not automatically reduce competition or raise prices. In fact, the opposite may even be the case. For this reason, it is necessary to show who actually suffers under a vertical agreement. When evaluating vertical restraints, it is necessary to consider the consequences in different ways. There is a need to show where harm may occur and, explicitly, who exactly is harmed' Haucap and Klein (2012, p. 180) (translated from German).

6.3 Opportunities for Cartel-Law Deregulation of Consumer-Goods Distribution

The question at issue is hypothetical: What could or would happen if all forms of vertical price coordination in the intra-brand area between manufacturing and retailing enterprises, and in the extreme, also the inflexible fixed-price maintenance system, were completely unregulated?

The Vertical Block Exemption Regulation of the European Commission and the Guidelines on Vertical Restraints (paragraph 225) do accept *some (but few) efficiency advantages of price restraints* that could justify individual exemption from the price-maintenance prohibition.[4] It is worth noting that even the European Commission generally assumes that *inter*-brand competition is more important than *intra*-brand competition. However, the question arises as to why the *multitude of much more significant efficiency advantages repeatedly cited by management theorists and business agents,* that could be brought about by the consistent deregulation of vertical marketing, are tenaciously ignored in cartel-law practice. The issues to be considered include.

6.3.1 The Liberation of System Competition from Structural Distortions

The main pro-competition effect of the deregulation of vertical marketing is the elimination of arguably one of the greatest risks to 'competition as a process of discovery'. This risk arises because distribution systems are forced by the State into forms of organisation that are economically suboptimal. The systematic structural distortion resulting from the *unequal legal treatment of the differing business models or forms of distribution* is, in itself reason enough to initiate deregulation without delay. What is meant is that many cartel-law restrictions affect free and cooperative forms of distribution and obstruct their free development, but not hierarchically controlled value systems. Vertically integrated groups of companies, multi-level chain-store systems and commission-agent and commercial-agent systems (e.g., in the mineral-oil sector) are permitted to do many things that cooperating and free distribution systems are currently strictly prohibited from doing. These include multi-level price management; there are no price restraints in hierarchical structures.

---

[4] Alongside short-term special-offer campaigns in cooperative distribution systems in which the maximum possible advertising impact is achieved by means of uniformly favourable prices, and combating the free-rider problem for products requiring in-depth advice, particular attention is drawn to the case of the market launch of a new product. In this context the manufacturer can, by means of the price tie, acquire distributors for market entry and, therefore, for investment in sales-promotional measures. Cf. European Commission (2010).

6.3.2 Raising Efficiency by Means of Free Communication, Cooperation and a Division of Labour Within the Vale Chain

Most of the efficiency gains are not directly (and therefore causally) attributable to the abolition of price-maintenance prohibition, but merely indirectly, and are no less economically relevant. This is because the abolition of this prohibition would render obsolete *an entire canon of supplementary regulations* generated over the last few years by the European Commission, the competition authorities and the courts for the purpose of interpreting vague legal concepts *that supplement the actual price maintenance prohibition*. The recommendation ('Handreichung') of the Federal Cartel Office, Germany, in which many modes of conduct usual in retailing practice are classified as suspicious for cartel-law purposes, also refers to these supplementary restrictions on commercial freedom of action in the area of vertical marketing. This tight network of rules appears overly bureaucratic and largely superfluous from a business perspective, because they cause more harm in public-policy terms than they create benefits, and the legal uncertainty associated with them is unacceptable to companies.

Since 2010, numerous companies have abandoned their practice-proven inter-level cooperation projects such as vertical category management, because of (real or possibly only inferred) threats posed by cartel law. This is highly regrettable from the points of view of competition and welfare, because such combined concepts of industry and commerce encourage innovation and are widely accepted by consumers. Moreover, necessary brand strategy coordination in the value chain is increasingly being abandoned, e.g., with respect to the desired target positioning for the branded article and the shops stocking them, because this *could* trigger suspicions of concerted price structuring and lead to an investigation. 'Liberating' business practice from this *hopelessly dense network of regulations on price-maintenance prohibition* can be described as another great opportunity for deregulation, not only for participants in free and cooperative value systems, but also for consumers in particular.

6.3.3 Innovative Services and Strong Brands as a Consequence of Liberating Value Processes

Consumers benefit from the greatest conceivable degree of welfare when the effectiveness of competition *between* competing supply concepts is assured over the long run. This presupposes supply diversity. Well-proven and innovative price-performance combinations compete with each other for consumer acceptance. Value systems in the consumer-goods sector are normally multi-level and the most attractive supply concepts often feature a harmonious 'composition' of excellent goods and services by manufacturers and distributors. Inconsistencies within such multi-level supply concepts, whether in brand communications or even strategic price positioning, may confuse consumers and reduce their faith in the quality. Deregulation would enable manufacturing and retailing enterprises to take the initiative themselves and, with appropriate price and brand maintenance, not only avoid upsetting consumers, but also trigger *considerable positive competition and welfare effects*.

These can be categorised into three closely-related sets of combined effects.

6.3.3.1 Development and Stabilisation of Strong Brands

For a strong brand to develop, a harmonious coordination of branding communication and price management in the sales channels is required. Modern marketing research shows that uncoordinated price-policy operations can harm, or even destroy the majority of strong brands, especially for goods and services of high-quality, which have a sensitive image or which require detailed advice. The legal system offers no effective protection against such dangers. If the owner of the brand is then also prohibited from taking action in the form of price maintenance, to *protect his brand against erosion*, he forfeits consumer demand. The brand pales into insignificance and *diversity is sacrificed* if consumers are forced unnecessarily to forego a desired consumption option. Without strong brands, consumer welfare is diminished.

6.3.3.2 Investment Incentives to Create and Launch Innovative Supply Concepts

Businesspeople invest in innovation only if they anticipate that:

- the supply concepts created can reach the consumer in unadulterated form, i.e., are not immediately caught up in price wars or become loss-leaders in retailing,
- the value partners can be motivated and urged to invest in supportive sales policy measures, because they are guaranteed sustainable margins,
- the opportunity to develop a strong brand does actually exist, i.e., there is no danger that the competition authorities will massively intervene against every form of vertical price and brand maintenance that is indispensable for branding to occur.

The argument repeatedly raised, that price maintenance leads to sluggish competition and reduces in a sector, is untenable in its claim of general validity. It can claim validity only in the extreme scenario of insurmountable barriers to market entry (i.e., high protective fences for obsolete products). In the normal case, the willingness to innovate and the dynamics of innovation are driven by, and not inhibited by vertical price management. The 'liberation of value processes from cartel-law restraints' *eliminates potential disturbances* that can be found *in all four subprocesses of the product and procedural progress* (i.e., mutation, selection, self-imitation and third-party imitation) and which are closely related to each other.

For example, foreseeable difficulties in the future with respect to the dissemination of an innovative product, possibly based on a lack of cooperation on the part of the target distribution group, may have a very negative effect on *industry willingness to mutate.* A distributor's lack of willingness to cooperate may, in turn, be traced back to his bad experiences with the conduct of fellow distributors within the same value system. Loss-leader offers, confusing signals from sales personnel, inadequate goods presentation etc. can cause *consumers to doubt the quality*, with the result of sensitively disrupting the selection process. Consequently, the possibility of *any strong brand formation* in the minds of customers (both consumers and distributors) is excluded from the outset. Finally, the possible *chain reaction of mutually propagating effects* already foreseeable ex ante, discourages manufacturers and distributors from making any investment whatsoever in complex processes of innovation.

The task of competition policy is to create parameters that enable innovators *to take action themselves* to ensure that the supply concepts that they consider likely to reach consumers unadulterated. Coordination processes within value systems, also explicitly measures of *vertical brand protection and multi-level price maintenance,* should be admissible in principle, to the extent to which they promote the efficient operation of innovation processes. If, on the contrary, an efficient influence by innovators on *intra*-brand multiplication is legally inadmissible, there is a risk that no change processes occur, because entrepreneurs place more value on the risk of losing the necessary 'return on investment' than on the opportunities associated with innovation. This creates a serious defect in *inter*-brand competition, a deficit which would normally have to be eliminated by competition-policy intervention, but which is in fact caused by the cartel-law regulation of vertical marketing.

6.3.3.3 Preservation and Extension of Established Supply Concepts

Not only the ongoing development and dissemination of *new* products, but—provided consumers display their preferences through their selection behaviour—an extension of the *established* range of products and, therefore, also the *stabilisation of strong brands* could likewise be the result of competition as a process of discovery. There are close interdependencies between these two processes; the undistorted marketing of proven supply concepts and the introduction of new products. This is because businesspeople would then be faced with a high risk of brand erosion—inevitable because their hands are tied by cartel law—right from the outset, this could stifle willingness to invest and therefore, efforts at innovation. Moreover, the impairment of ongoing business success owing to a lack of 'sustainable' margins—at both manufacturing and retail levels—can in turn prevent the release of investment funds urgently needed for innovation. Destroying incentives for innovation in this way is surely *one of the most dangerous market distortions.*

6.3.4 Promoting Supply Diversity by Means of Competing Price-Formation Methods

The demand for a diversity of supply concepts that are unrestricted as far as possible, also expressly applies to *freedom of choice in vertical price-structuring processes*. If the consumer were allowed to choose, for example, between products with autonomously structured prices or recommended prices, with concerted prices or tied prices, this could provide greater ‘welfare’ than if he was denied this opportunity to choose. The requirement for this welfare gain, however, is *effective competition between the alternative price-formation variations*. If price-maintenance prohibition were to be abolished, this could give rise to a price-policy heterogeneity that is highly attractive to the consumer.

Here are just a few examples:

- Some of the competing supply concepts find favour with consumers because their prices change constantly. This may suit those consumers set on seeking variety or finding bargains. *Ongoing price variations* can be controlled centrally, in which case the branded article manufacturer or headquarters of a branched distribution system can assume the control function, as in the case of trademarks. Price formation can also be left to the free play of market forces within the value system.
- Many consumers place a high value on *price consistency*, either for example to ensure that the value of a gift does not decline, because of conspicuous consumption or the snob effect, or quite simply because they do not wish to be upset at having earlier paid too high a price.
- Numerous value systems are characterised by the fact that distributors at no time want to be deprived of sovereignty over price structuring, even if price restraints were allowed. In this context, price-formation processes therefore *focus on distributors*.
- Other business models are successful, particularly because it is not the local retailer but the wholesaler of a cooperative retail group, the franchisor or even the manufacturer who undertakes *professional price management centrally*, thereby relieving those at the front line of the difficult business of calculating prices.
- It may make economic sense for the fundamental price positioning of a branded article to be the subject of a *strategic agreement* between industry and commerce, while the *operative fine-tuning* is decentralised.
- Many distributors place great value on *guidance from recommended prices*, while others need or desire no such assistance. Recommended prices can also be a valuable aid for consumers.

These examples clearly show the diversity of ‘customer-oriented solutions’ that could emerge from competition as a process of discovery, if it were not restricted by cartel law. The prohibition of resale price maintenance considerably limits this range of alternatives, reducing the consumption options preferred by consumers (e.g., prices for ‘his’ brands that are uniform and/or stable over time).

6.4 Principles of Partial Deregulation on a Case-by-Case Approach

The abovementioned positive effects of the deregulation of vertical marketing have long been familiar in business economics, and in marketing especially. It is remarkable that, except for the efficiency potential mentioned in the Vertical Block Exemption Regulations and in the Guidelines on Vertical Restraints, these advantages have been stubbornly ignored in the cartel-law debate. By contrast, advocates of strict price-maintenance prohibition refer to serious anti-competitive effects of vertical price coordination and do so on the basis of theoretical assumptions. The need to use models is explained by the fact that there is almost no experience with operation of price restraints, as they have been prohibited in most countries (with some exceptions) for so long. Therefore, it is possible only to speculate or theorise.

6.4.1 Risks of Free Price-Formation Processes Within the Value Chain

There are essentially two categories of assumed effects which, depending on the circumstances, could provide legitimate arguments against the deregulation of price-maintenance prohibition:

1. The risk that vertical price agreements could encourage the formation and entrenchment of horizontal price cartels.
2. The risk that consumer welfare could be impaired by excessive and inflexible prices as a consequence of legally permissible price-maintenance systems.

The common factor of the numerous hypotheses we have shown above, is that anti-competitive or welfare-reducing effects are attributed largely to the *inflexible systems of a fixed-price restraint which is identical for all buyers in tight oligopolies*. For this reason, issuing risk warnings is largely a waste of time because, according to our most recent empirical research, the overwhelming majority of branded-article manufacturers do not regard inflexible fixed-price maintenance systems as a desirable price strategy and the majority of retail enterprises categorically reject them. There are plenty of reasons why manufacturers and distributors have no interest in vertical price maintenance on a contractual basis, even if it is legally admissible. Of particular importance are the high costs of the introduction and ongoing price-guarantee system of vertical price maintenance, the lack of flexibility of price management, the risk of high market-share losses in functioning markets, i.e., with adequate and reasonable alternatives for consumers, damage to image if fair price conduct is called into question and, not least, the lack of enforceability among retail enterprises.

Therefore, in manufacturing and retailing practice, it is almost never a question of re-introducing resale price maintenance but, at most, of taking precautions within the value systems to make it possible to prevent, or at least mitigate, the crudest forms of conduct of some participants. Marketing experts are of the opinion that vertical price and brand care and efficiency-oriented vertical cooperation should be possible without immediately being forced into the tight corset of a wholly inflexible fixation of uniform point prices.

6.4.2 The Case-by-Case Approach: Limiting the Prohibition of Price Restraints to Certain Critical Situations

Given the largely pro-competitive effects of vertical price coordination in the normal case, there appears to be an urgent need at the present time to *abolish the per-se prohibition* of price restraints. A differentiating rule which limits a prohibition statute to certain critical situations is referred to as a *case-by-case* approach. It may also be considered a deregulation compromise. What 'critical situations' could be meant in this case? The decisive factor is the existence of a substantial risk to the effectiveness of *inter*-brand competition. Negative effects may appear in the cases characterised as follows:

- essential goods that are urgently needed,
- markets that are completely stagnant and barely innovative,
- almost insurmountable barriers to market entry.

Under the principle of effective market processes, such circumstances could justifiably be referred to as a *'nightmare scenario of complete market failure'*. This represents the first case where the need to retain the prohibition of price maintenance appears clear and compelling. However, even in such an extreme situation, it is questionable whether the price restraint can be revealed to be the *cause* of market failure or whether the imposition of price-maintenance prohibition can be regarded as merely treating *the symptoms*.

When defining the 'critical situations', however, consideration must be given not only to a situation of complete market failure. Additionally, a prohibition, or at least a special examination for the purpose of abuse control (rule-of-reason approach), could also be considered, if individual risk factors existed (in the sense of assumptions capable of being disproved), for example, in the case of:

- market-dominating companies as initiators of inflexible fixed resale price maintenance systems (these companies were prohibited from introducing a price-maintenance system even before 1973),
- markets with a very high market share of price-tied products, e.g., more than 50 %,
- a market structure with a high probability of collusive behaviour,
- situations in which the desire for price maintenance emanates from distributors.

It is obvious that these cases require more in-depth economic discussion. In general, the following conclusions appear at least worthy of discussion.

If the *competition processes of a particular market are proven effective*, there is absolutely no justification for cartel-law intervention in the value processes. In this case, the prohibition of vertical price maintenance is fundamentally misguided.

If, instead, market effectiveness is distorted, the *causes of market failure* must be analysed and remedied using competition policy. As a rule *excessively high barriers to market entry* ultimately cause market failure. Vertical coordination in the form of price and brand maintenance will *not normally create* insurmountable barriers to market entry. Rather, the admissibility of vertical price coordination *can help to break down* market entry barriers by means of innovative supply concepts.

It may become dangerous for the effectiveness of competition in *tight oligopoly markets* if *inflexible fixed-price maintenance systems gain a very large market share*. Only then can removing the price-maintenance prohibition have negative effects on horizontal inter-brand competition under certain circumstances—in particular by promoting price cartels. Although, in the event of increasing market coverage with price-maintained goods, consumers would increasingly wish to switch to non-price-maintained products, they could not do so if there were almost insurmountable barriers to market entry. If consumers were also unable to abstain from buying (e.g., *essential goods*) then, and only then, should the strict regulation of vertical price coordination in the value chain be considered as a last competition-policy resort.

A minimum requirement for the deregulation of consumer-goods distribution is that the special status of vertical price maintenance as *hardcore restraints (Kernbeschränkungen)* in the block exemption regulations should be abolished. The fundamental exemptions in accordance with Art. 101 (3) TFEU should also apply to vertical price maintenance, because the commonly assumed risks of negative effects on inter-brand competition (e.g., the support of price cartels) do not normally exist. Only in cases of inflexible fixed-price restraints are harmful effects on the effectiveness of competitive processes even conceivable and, here too, only if companies that dominate the market are involved and if market coverage substantially exceeds 50 %.

References

Ahlert D (2012) The liberation of the value chain from cartel-law restraints', the risks and opportunities of deregulation. In: Zeitschrift für Vertriebsrecht 4/2012, pp 207–218

European Commission (2010) Guidelines on vertical restraints (Text with EEA relevance) (2010/C 130/01)

Haucap J, Klein G (2012) Einschränkungen der Preisgestaltung im Einzelhandel aus wettbewerbsökonomischer Perspektive. In: Ahlert D, Kenning P, Schröder H, Olbrich R (eds) Vertikale Preis- und Markenpflege im Kreuzfeuer des Kartellrechts, Wiesbaden, pp 169–186

Annex I

The provisional evaluation of practices in negotiations between manufacturers of branded articles, wholesalers and retail enterprises—Recommendation of the Federal Cartel Office (Germany) of 13 April 2010.

In connection with the investigation in the food industry in January 2010, the Federal Cartel Office (Germany) outlined its recommendation ('Handreichung') in a letter to companies which had made a bonus application in the course of the investigations, for the purpose of defining the duties of cooperation. The list contains firstly practices which (according to provisional evaluation) are normally inadmissible under cartel law, because they represent the agreement or coordination of *resale prices or (promotional) minimum price levels* in accordance with sec. 1 GWB and Art. 101 (1) TFEU or a *unilateral exercise of pressure or granting of advantages* to cause such an agreement or coordination as defined in sec. 21 (2) GWB.

On the other hand, the list contains practices which are not sufficient in themselves to constitute price maintenance or horizontal coordination. The same applies to practices which cannot in themselves be evaluated as a unilateral exercise of pressure or granting of advantages. Nevertheless, they may be indications and, in a general context or in combination with inadmissible practices, be regarded as measures promoting price stabilisation which are generally covered by the prohibition of vertical price maintenance or, if appropriate, an *indirect price agreement* between retail enterprises or the inadmissible exercise of pressure or granting of advantages.

The contents of the recommendation of *particular relevance for the present publication* are reproduced below in a shortened (only partially literal) version[1]:

1. **Price autonomy and economic risk**

Price competition in the trade with consumer goods is characterised by the fact that wholesale and retail companies set their own prices themselves, on the basis of

[1] Cf. on this and thereafter Federal Cartel Office (2010) (translated from German).

D. Ahlert and B. Schefer, *Vertical Price Coordination and Brand Care*, SpringerBriefs in Business, DOI: 10.1007/978-3-642-35570-7,

the negotiated manufacturer ex works prices and their own price policies, and themselves bear the economic risk of these policies.[2]

2. Concerted practices and communications

A concerted practice, as distinguished from a contractual agreement, would exist in each form of communication which, although it did not lead to the conclusion of a contract in the real sense, deliberately allowed practical cooperation instead of risk-related competition. This practical cooperation creates competition conditions that do not reflect normal market conditions. A supplier merely handing over a list with recommended resale prices to a retail enterprise that asked for the same does not constitute an act of vertical price maintenance. The supplier can also, when handing over this list, explain the reasons for the recommended prices and generally explain what strategy it pursues with regard to the positioning and marketing of its products. However, the recommendation must remain non-binding legally and in fact. Consequently, retail or wholesale companies may only then implement the same if they would do so on the basis of an autonomous decision. Making contact once, after sending on the recommended retail price (RRP) can suffice to enable the participating companies to coordinate their market behaviour.

3. Unilateral use of pressure and incentives

Cartel law may be infringed in vertical relationships, even if there has been no agreement or concerted behaviour. This is because the unilateral use of pressure and incentives to enforce vertical price restraints—whether by the supplier or by the distributor—can be a breach of sec. 21 (2) GWB. Slight pressure may already constitute an infringement.[3]

4. Price promotions and advertising support

Generally deemed to be inadmissible and non-exemptible are the written or verbal coordination or fixing (e.g., in annual agreements) of resale prices or (promotional) minimum price levels. The same applies to the support of advertising measures of the trade by product-related remuneration or flat-rate discounts on the

---

[2] In the case of each agreement and concerted practice between suppliers and retailers or wholesalers or between wholesalers and retailers in verbal or written form on the fixing of resale prices or (promotional) minimum price levels, this represents a *hardcore restraint of competition* in the opinion of the Federal Cartel Office. As a result, it is presumed that sec. 1 GWB/Art. 101(1) TFEU is met and that no exemption under sec. 2 (1) GWB / Art. 101(3) TFEU is possible.

[3] *Disadvantages* to the implementation of inadmissible price restraints may be, for example, penalties (e.g., unilateral deduction from invoices), delisting, deterioration of terms and conditions, termination, delay, suspension or limitation of deliveries, cancellation or reduction of promotions/placements/shelf space, distribution-channel restrictions. *Advantages* for the enforcement of inadmissible price restraints may be, for example, brand or price-maintenance discounts, promotional price supports, refunds, margin-equalization payments/receivables or the granting of other advantages by a supplier for adherence to a minimum retailer margin on the manufacturer's ex-works price.

part of the supplier, if specific promotional prices were required by one of the two contractual partners.

5. **Price recommendations and margin impartiality**

The stipulation of binding resale prices or minimum resale price levels by the supplier in pre-printed order forms, purchase orders or other documents and their unchanged use by retail companies in connection with procurement procedures would be deemed inadmissible. The same applies to agreements and coordinations between manufacturers and distributors regarding margin impartiality or improvement of margins in raising manufacturer ex-works prices, with simultaneously increasing of resale prices (sliding price maintenance).[4]

6. **Examples of dubious modes of conduct**

Examples of practices which in themselves according to the current viewpoint, do not constitute a breach of sec. 1 GWB, Art. 101 (1) TFEU or sec. 21 (2) GWB, but which, in a given context, could indicate an inadmissible practice, especially if they occur in concerted form, are those listed below:

- Making the resale price or a maximum possible undercutting of an RRP or another recommended resale or promotional price the subject of debate.
- The participation or involvement of retail enterprises in the systematic observation of resale prices by suppliers or in measures which could be understood as monitoring (price- monitoring systems).
- Compiling/elaborating or requesting price-comparison lists or collections of till receipts or other sensitive information of a competitive nature, for the purpose of transmission to companies on the opposing side of the market.
- The provision by manufacturers to wholesalers or retailers of aids to calculation or guides to sales-price calculation.
- Imprinting of RRP or adhesive labels with RRP on products of the manufacturer or the use of sales aids of the manufacturer with ready-made price details or RRP.
- Imprint of resale prices on packages or materials intended to show the price in the shop or their stipulation in advertising measures of the manufacturer without the indication 'Recommended retail price'.

7. **Horizontal effects and tripartite relations**

Vertical price restraints would normally have a horizontal effect on the price-setting behaviour of retailers. This may be the case where there is a tripartite

[4] In the opinion of the Cartel Office, price competition in the manufacture of and trade in consumer goods are characterised by the fact that companies of wholesale and retail trade themselves undertake margin calculations on the basis of the negotiated "net-net prices" and perform their own price policy and themselves bear the economic risk of their price policy. This means that retail enterprises can 'start off' at the selling prices of competitors if they do so on the basis of an autonomous decision and without direct or indirect contact and/or coordination with the competitors.

agreement between supplier and wholesaler/distributor (hub and spoke), if the communication of the retail companies via the supplier (indirectly) is aimed at or results in horizontal coordination of the prices or other competition parameters between the distributors. Normally deemed inadmissible by the decision-making department are practices such as the following:

- The partial or complete disclosure of the conditions or contracts that the supplier has agreed with a competing distributor.
- Most-favoured clauses or comparable verbal or written agreements aimed at a uniform price level in wholesaling or retailing.
- The transmission to other distributors, at their instigation, of price-related information gained by the supplier from its contractual relationships with a distributor.
- Distributors may not coordinate the selection, sales strategy or advertising with their suppliers, where this serves the purpose of direct or indirect coordination of such measures with other distributors. This also applies to the temporal coordination of promotions between distributors and suppliers, if they serve the above purpose.
- Offering or granting advantages or disadvantages tied to adherence to a recommended resale price or a minimum selling price level linked to adherence to this price or minimum price level by third parties. This covers, for example, the demands for compensation and settlement amounts, invoice deductions and guaranteed margins for distributors if the resale prices recommended by a supplier are not implemented by other distributors in the market.

8. **Other critical modes of conduct with horizontal effects**

Other examples of measures, whose practice in themselves do not constitute a breach of sec. 1 GWB, Art. 101 (1) TFEU, but which, in the certain contexts, could indicate inadmissible practice:

- The communication of or complaints to the supplier about the resale prices of competitors observed in the market.
- The participation of retail enterprises in monitoring resale prices by suppliers as well as, vice versa, the participation of suppliers in measures to monitor selling prices by distributors.

Annex II

Vertical price and brand maintenance—terminological and typological basis—(author: Benjamin Schefer)

> 'We are always talking about the same thing: I talk about price maintenance and you talk about price care and brand management. [...] We are of the opinion that, as soon as the manufacturer has parted with the product, the distributor is free in setting his price—that is how it is also seen by law. This is the law under the GWB and it is also European law. [...] I would like to have a definition for these two words (author's note: price care and brand care) [...]. What is the difference, is that price maintenance? If it's not, what is it then?' (Andreas Mundt, President of the Federal Cartel Office at the Congress 'Wettbewerb im Handel' (Competition in Commerce) in the CDU/CSU party parliamentary meeting room in the German Bundestag on 30 November 2011).

Since the start of investigations into vertical price agreements in the food trade, a lively discussion has again developed in Germany about the sense and nonsense of the current cartel-law provisions and their interpretation. There is regular discourse between academics, businesspersons and the legal enforcement bodies (especially the Federal Cartel Office); attempts have been made at numerous symposia, congresses and podium discussions since then to find solutions in this matter. As shown by the congress 'Competition in Commerce' of the CDU/CSU political parties on 30 November 2011, progress based on consensus frequently fails, due to a lack of a commonly understood concept of price care and brand care or price care and brand management (see also the opening quotation from Andreas Mundt).[5] The following statements are intended to shed light on these concepts and thereby create a constructive basis for future progress in this field. For this purpose, it makes sense to divide the concept of 'price care and brand care' into its constituent parts. The word 'brand' is of central significance. The importance of a brand for the success of a product has been proven in numerous investigations.[6] At this point, I refer only to

[5] Any potential difference between brand management and brand care in this article should be ignored; any knowledge gained in this respect would be of a merely theoretical nature at this point. For this reason, the terms should initially be understood as synonyms for definitional purposes.

[6] See also Annex 1II.

D. Ahlert and B. Schefer, *Vertical Price Coordination and Brand Care*, SpringerBriefs in Business, DOI: 10.1007/978-3-642-35570-7,

the most famous study on brand perception by De Chernatony and McDonald (2003), which revealed the relevance of given brand information for the decision to purchase as part of a so-called 'blind test'.[7] In the experiment, consumers had to sample two different types of diet cola and evaluate them in terms of their preferred taste. Without any brand indication, 51 % of the test participants preferred *Pepsi*. In a control group with a comparable composition of test persons, but with openly communicated brand information, only 23 % of the participants favoured *Pepsi-Cola*, whereas 65 % preferred *Coca-Cola*. Clearly, the brand *Coca-Cola* conveys additional value to consumers that they subconsciously include in their decision-making behaviour. Even it has not yet been possible to quantify the precise asset value of a brand for a company or the brand strength itself, there is no dispute in theory or practice about the considerable contribution made by a strong brand to the success of a company.[8]
As a consequence, recourse should be made to the brand concept of Ahlert and Ahlert (Handbuch Franchising und Cooperation: Das Management kooperativer Unternehmensnetzwerke, 2010), which was developed through interdisciplinary discourse between economists and brand experts from the industry[9]:

> 'Brands are collective interpretative patterns that people use as guides to settle conflicts by means of decisions. Brands arise anthropologically from the processing of complex experiences. Brand creation takes place unconsciously, unavoidably and continuously and is exposed to many uncontrolled influences.
> The structure of a brand consists of a varying image and an invariable essence. The brand essence that represents its true value is rooted largely in the unconscious. To this extent, it cannot be documented by means of opinion or image research, but can be localised by brain research and anthropological psychology'.[10]

The authors use seven sub-statements to explain this definition that should apply equally to the concept of brand care as a means of understanding the brand.

1. A brand forms in the human psyche and is not 'made' by advertising agencies or company head offices. However, its formation can be deliberately influenced.
2. Brand creation is based on noteworthy products or services.
3. An achievement is worth noting if it represents a solution to a problem for a person, e.g., makes it easier to choose between alternatives.
4. The development of the brand takes place in interaction with all members of the brand public, which consists of the capital market, sales market, personnel market, procurement market, sales agency/partner market and the public.
5. Over the course of time, the brand develops independently of the product or company, so that it can even outlive the real achievements originally associated it. A brand exists as a 'fiction in people's minds'.

---

[7] Cf. on this and thereafter de Chernatony and McDonald (2003, pp. 14f).

[8] Cf. examplarily Köster (2006, p. 30f) and Ahlert and Ahlert (2010, pp. 374ff).

[9] Cf. on this and thereafter Ahlert and Ahlert (2010, pp. 363ff).

[10] Ahlert and Ahlert (2010, p. 365) (translated from German).

6. Brands are influenced by all departments of the companies, as well as external reference groups (e.g., sales agents, advertising agencies, etc.). The task of market-oriented management consists of coordinating all these influences with a view to the brand-policy aims.
7. Brand image is variable; in contrast the brand essence rooted in the subconscious, which is invariable. Accordingly, the latter is much more significant for the strength of a brand.

In a second stage, we seek to understand the word 'care'. In the German language, this describes 'treatment with the necessary means to preserve a good condition' (Duden 2011). If this definition is used in a specific context, it raises the question of how to characterise the specific, well-regarded condition and what measures are required to preserve it. By reference to brand care, the good condition to be preserved should be equated with preserving the brand concept as elaborated by a branded-article manufacturer. This specifically means the building and preservation of brand essence in the minds of individual members of the brand public, because it is they who mainly determine brand strength. The variable of brand image in its different states should always match the brand essence, in order to avoid upsetting consumers and endangering the brand. This harmonisation and the coordination of other diverse influences with respect to the brand-policy should take place through the marketing mix, which mainly determines the brand concept.

The marketing mix includes the use of specific marketing instruments with varied intensity from the areas of product policy, distribution policy, price policy and communications policy, in order to achieve defined marketing aims.[11] A manufacturer of branded articles cannot use different instruments independently of each other, firstly because of budget restrictions and secondly, of particular importance, because of interdependencies between the sub-areas of the marketing mix. According to Meffert et al. (2012), taking account of these interdependencies is of central importance in structuring the marketing mix, because the relevant functional, temporal and hierarchical dependencies between the individual elements can decisively promote or endanger the efficiency and effectiveness of the entire mix.[12]

The following discussion will focus particularly on price policy, as it appears to be affected primarily and potentially at risk from current cartel law and its interpretation. Nevertheless, because of the interactions indicated above, the other areas of the marketing mix cannot be ignored; price policy especially is strongly influenced, for example, by measures in other marketing dimensions, as will become evident in due course.

Based on the definition of the word 'care' given above, price care can be understood as preserving the price conceptions of the manufacturer. The interpretation of this concept implies that brand care—in accordance with the

[11] Cf. Meffert et al. (2012, p. 786). For a detailed presentation of different types of dependency, cf. Meffert et al. (2012, pp. 787f).

[12] Cf. Meffert et al. (2012, p. 787).

considerations explained above—represents the outer framework within which the measures of price care take place. Finally, price care, as a sub-area of manufacturer-driven brand care, simultaneously serves the overall aim of preserving the brand concept. Selecting the optimum price in economic terms, of an adequate price corridor or, expressed in general terms, the development of the product-specific price conception does not therefore entail price care, but precedes it.

Nevertheless, this view can only correctly present one side of the phenomenon of price care. In no other dimension of the marketing mix is the realisation of the concept so strongly dependent on the acts of another party with partially conflicting interests. In the vertical distribution systems between manufacturing and retailing under consideration here, the distributor has the last word in fixing the final consumer price, because of the right to price sovereignty. Because of the wide range of brands offered, his aggregate profit does not depend on the radiating effect of one single manufacturer's brand, but is more strongly defined by his own store-brand profile.[13] Consequently, the building and preservation of the brand essence has merely secondary importance from the distributor's point of view; the same applies to the preservation of the former's price conceptions. Nevertheless, the interests of each of the parties do not diverge completely. A distributor may benefit from preserving the price-policy conceptions of the manufacturer, if they yield adequate income for the distributor through ultimate viable final consumer price which is compatible with the distributor's own price policy and is achievable *in the free competition of the distribution systems*. Price care from the point of view of the distributor is, for this reason, considered hereafter as being equivalent to maintenance one's *own price-policy* by reference to the final price of a branded article which, reflecting the considerations manufacturers outlined above should be consistent with the remainder of one's *own marketing mix*. The specific combination of interests, depending on the organisation of the commercial system (e.g., full-range trader or discounter) and of the marketing mix of the manufacturer, should be evaluated only case by case (see Fig. A.1).

For the reasons given above, a distinction should be made between *price care from the perspective of the distributor* as explained above and *price care from a manufacturer's point of view*.

The *manufacturer's perspective* is now subjected to closer inspection. In order to achieve a more specific definition of the relatively abstract term so as to achieve a better understanding, the measures associated with price care are characterised and located. One approach to this is offered by the following Fig. A.2. As shown in the figure, price care measures can be defined in a three-way relationship consisting of branded-article manufacturer, distributor and consumer. An in-depth understanding of price care and brand care can be gained only from an overall view of all relevant relationships represented.

---

[13] Cf. examplarily Ahlert and Kenning (2007, pp. 157ff).

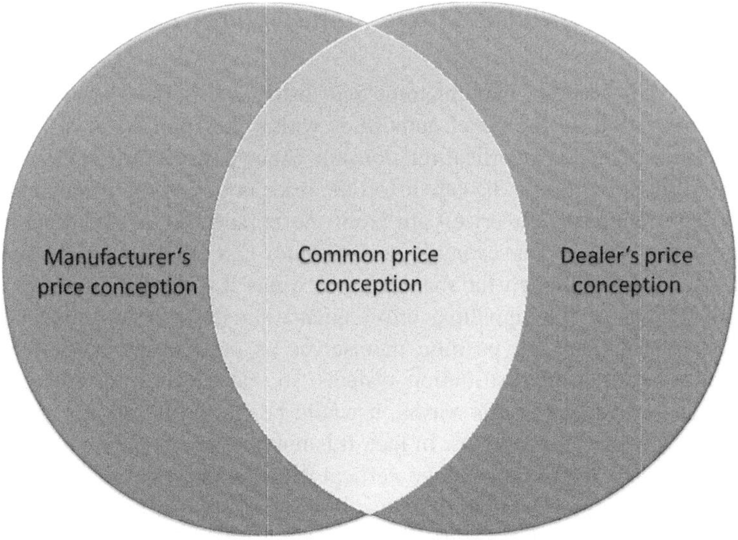

Fig. A.1 Pricing interests of manufacturers and retailers

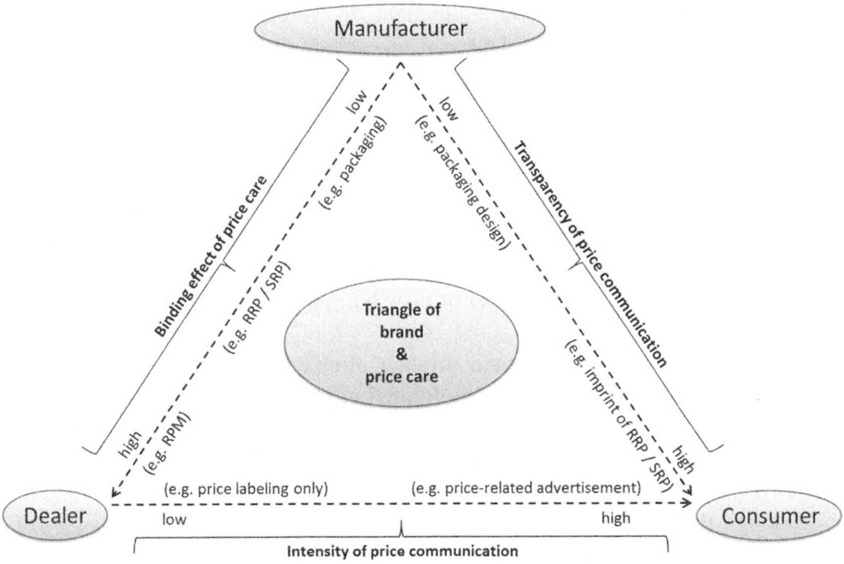

Fig. A2 Triangle of (brand and) price care

Relationship of Branded-Article Manufacturer to Distributor

The relationship between manufacturer and distributor is particularly subject to critical observation by the cartel authorities within the framework of price care, also described below as a vertical relationship. Since a distributor in Germany has the right to set prices freely, he can distort the price policy of the manufacturer (cf. also the considerations on price care from the perspective of the manufacturer outlined earlier above) For example, a distributor can label an article as a low-priced loss-leader, although the manufacturer wants it to be positioned at a high price. By means of the signalling effect emanating from price-setting conduct, individual distributors can position themselves as particularly cost-effective in competition between the distribution systems, so that a strong incentive towards such conduct prevails. For this reason, it would be correct to talk not only of the preservation of price conceptions. In fact, it is not possible to implement the price policy without the distributors in the vertical distribution systems.

How can a branded-article manufacturer now influence the price-setting conduct of a distributor? Corresponding measures can be classified on a continuum in terms of their binding effect: Such a measure is not especially binding for the distributors, if their leeway for decision-making is not restricted in any way by the manufacturer. At the same time, the precise aim of the manufacturers to limit this leeway for decision-making is equivalent to motivating the distributor to implement their price policies. This can take place either through of persuasion (rational from a business point of view) or by force (questionable from the cartel-law point of view). Vertical price care takes place in a particularly subtle and thus non-binding manner, without direct communication of the target selling price, but using other surrogates that convey the price conceptions of the manufacturer. Conceivable, for example, is a particularly high-quality design for a single article such as a bottle for sparkling wine with a sophisticated design. Equally conceivable are other measures of product policy, communication policy (e.g., price-related advertising, see below) or distribution policy (e.g., the selection of a trading partner).

The ex-works price of a certain product already has a more binding effect, because selling below cost price is prohibited at least pro forma in Germany and would also not be worthwhile in individual cases. The infinite freedom to set prices in a thought experiment where there are no price-care measures is sensibly restricted from a business point of view by the above considerations.

Although the recommended retail price—as the word implies—is merely of a suggestion and the distributor, in accordance with German law, is completely free to set prices, it must be positioned more centrally within the continuum. The range for setting final consumer prices is narrowed and the binding effect increases as soon as the price recommendation is communicated not only to distributors but also to consumers. This can take place, for example, by printing the RRP on the product packaging. In this way, the consumer develops a corresponding price conception which, in the majority of cases, prevents a sale above the RRP. The binding effect of this measure may increase further, depending on how strongly and how frequently the price recommendation is communicated to the consumer. But this depends not only on the measure itself, but also on the environment, e.g., the negotiating power of the two parties. One example of the increased communication of the recommended retail price is the project *Varta rettet die Marge* (Varta rescues the margin), which conveys the target price position to the retail sector in advertisements and on a detailed website with the aid of ten so-called *margin rules*.

The most binding measure for distributors would consist of linking final consumer prices, which is prohibited in Germany. However, a distinction is still required as to whether this concerns merely a bilaterally negotiated binding agreement that does not cover the entire business sector and can very easily be structured differently with other distributors, or whether it concerns a sector-wide inflexible fixed-price restraint. There is currently dissension in Germany with regard to the classification of vertical price-care measures or the entire vertical price-care programme of a manufacturer on this 'bindingness' continuum. As a guide for the companies affected by the investigation of vertical price agreements, the Federal Cartel Office has published a provisional recommendation (Handreichung) which distinguishes between clearly prohibited situations and practices that could possibly be classified as legally critical.[14] The legality of the latter can be ascertained only in an overall evaluation of all measures, so that this recommendation has been unable to create a safe harbour until now.

Relationship of Branded-Article Manufacturer to Consumer

The manufacturer of branded goods is concerned with persuading consumers of his own price conception and internalising, in their purchasing behaviour, a corresponding willingness to pay for the product of the manufacturer. Corresponding measures can be located on a continuum which describes the transparency of communications of the firm's own price conception. As already outlined in the relationship between branded-article manufacturer and distributor, the packaging of a product may itself evoke price associations (cf. the sophisticated design of a bottle for sparkling wine). Because, in this case, no specific price level is specified, the price conception is conveyed more implicitly. Comparable effects on consumers could be exerted by further product-policy, communications-policy (e.g., television advertising) or distribution-policy measures (e.g., sale by selected specialist distributors). A combination of the various measures consolidates the price image, with the effect that the consumer himself tends to gain a clearer idea of the price.

---

[14] Cf. Annex I of this publication.

However, the manufacturer can also clearly and unequivocally communicate the ultimate consumer prices he conceives for his product to the consumer. An individual measure of this kind would be, for example, explicit communication of the recommended retail price (e.g., by printing it on the article itself). Particularly transparent in price communications would be behaviour on the part of a manufacturer, which consists not only of openly communicating the RRP, but also conveying a correspondingly synchronised price image in all marketing dimensions.

Relationship of Distributor to Consumer

Not to be ignored is the relationship between distributor and consumer because, ultimately, this is where consumer prices are 'formed' and also where the effects or results of price care become obvious. But even after a final price setting, the role of individual distributors within the framework of price care is not merely passive. Depending on the intensity with which price setting is communicated, the individual price knowledge that comprises all price information in the mind of an individual consumer[15] is influenced. This may affect both explicit price knowledge in the form of specific prices able to be recalled for certain articles, but also the implicit price knowledge that is more equivalent to a diffuse, uncertain feeling or such a conception of the price level.[16] The explicit price knowledge of consumers for the majority of articles is not very high, as various studies have demonstrated.[17] Consumers have a good knowledge of prices only for a small selection of strongly-branded articles. No intensive price communication by the distributor is required for consumers to consciously acknowledge the prices set. These normally involve reference articles on the basis of which the consumer judges the price image of the shop's entire range. Since these have a correspondingly high acquisitorial potential, they are normally advertised strongly with the aid of the final price. For all other articles, the consumer does not immediately register the relevant price label, for which reason the intensity of price communication in this case should be regarded as low.

Where competition between distribution systems is highly developed, high-intensity communication of the set price influences the price-setting behaviour of other distributors and, therefore, ultimately, also leads to adjustment of the price policy of the manufacturer. For example, when stressing an extremely low consumer price for a branded article positioned at a high price, using low-quality and low-cost advertising, this may endanger the brand concept, because of the interdependencies described earlier.

---

[15] Cf. Pechtl (2005, p. 1).

[16] Cf. Ahlert et al. (2006, p. 11) and Monroe et al. (1986, p. 598).

[17] Cf. Dickson and Sawyer (1990), Evanschitzky et al. (2004) and Ahlert et al. (2006).

Conclusion

Only the overall view of the various measures described regarding the tripartite relations between branded-article manufacturer, distributor and consumer can guarantee an adequate understanding of brand and price care.

In summary, brand care means preserving of the market concept of the manufacturer or developing and preserving the brand essence using the appropriate measures. These include price care which, in relation to the final price of a branded article, help to preserve the price conception acquired in the course of the marketing mix, either of the manufacturer or the distributor, depending on which perspective is used in the analysis. Only integrating both these points of view can convey a comprehensive understanding of price care.

Given the interdependencies between the individual subareas of the marketing mix, the care measures cannot be viewed separately. Although the statements in the book containing the original German version of this article[18] focus on the price components, we knowingly refer to both brand and price as care. The specific developments in *vertical* brand and price care are analysed here, which refer primarily to the relations between branded-article manufacturers and distributors.

References

Ahlert D, Ahlert M (2010) Netzgeführte Marken: Markenmanagement in Unternehmensnetzwerken. In: Ahlert D, Ahlert M (eds) Handbuch Franchising und Cooperation: Das Management kooperativer Unternehmensnetzwerke. Frankfurt am Main, pp 361–381

Ahlert, D.; Kenning, P. (2007) Handelsmarketing: Grundlagen der marktorientierten Führung von Handelsbetrieben, Berlin

Ahlert D, Hartleb V, Eberhardt, T, Kenning P (2006) Messung von Preiswissen – ein Methodenvergleich, Survey, Westfälische Wilhelms-University, Muenster

Ahlert D, Kenning P, Schröder H, Olbrich R (eds) (2012) Vertikale Preis- und Markenpflege im Kreuzfeuer des Kartellrechts, Wiesbaden.

De Chernatony L, McDonald M (2003) Creating powerful brands in consumer, service and industrial markets, 3rd edn. Oxford, Elsevier

Dickson PR, Sawyer AG (1990) The price knowledge and search of supermarket shoppers. J Mark 54(3):42–53

Evanschitzky H, Kenning P, Vogel V (2004) Consumer price knowledge in the German retail market. J Prod Brand Manage 13(6):390–405

Federal Cartel Office (Bundeskartellamt) (2010) Vorläufige Bewertung von Verhaltensweisen in Verhandlungen zwischen Herstellern von Markenartikeln, Großhändlern und Einzelhandelsunternehmen zum Zwecke der Konkretisierung der Kooperationspflichten. In: Wirtschaft und Wettbewerb, Jg. 60, Nr. 07/08, S. 786–791

Köster L. (2006) Markenstärkemessung unter besonderer Berücksichtigung von Konsumentenheterogenität: Das Beispiel der deutschen Brauwirtschaft, Wiesbaden

[18] Cf. Ahlert et al. (2012).

Meffert H, Burmann C, Kirchgeorg M (2012) Marketing: Grundlagen marktorientierter Unternehmensführung. Konzepte—Instrumente—Praxisbeispiele, 11, revised and extended edition, Wiesbaden

Monroe KB, Powell CP, Choudhury PK (1986) Recall versus recognition as a measure of price awareness. Adv Consum Res 13(1):594-599

Pechtl H (2005) Preispolitik, Stuttgart

The manufacturer's authorised representative in the EU is Springer Nature Customer Service Centre GmbH, Europaplatz 3, 69115 Heidelberg, Germany. If you have any concerns regarding our products, please contact ProductSafety@springernature.com

Printed and bound by CPI Group (UK) Ltd, Croydon, CR0 4YY
01/10/2026
02225981-0007